D0287447

Be a Better Writer
POWER TOOLS FOR YOUNG WRITERS!

Essential Tips, Exercises and Techniques for Aspiring Writers

STEVE PEHA
MARGOT CARMICHAEL LESTER

www.leveragefactory.com

Essential Tips, Exercises and Techniques for Aspiring Writers

Be a Better Writer

POWER TOOLS FOR YOUNG WRITERS!

STEVE PEHA | MARGOT CARMICHAEL LESTER

www.beawriter.US

check it out!

Be a Better Writer—Power Tools for Young Writers!

Published by	The Leverage Factory, Inc.
Authors	Steve Peha & Margot Carmichael Lester
Development	The Word Factory
Copy	Charlotte Cox Communications
Layout	Anny B. Thompson
Design	Pete Minnelli & Anny B. Thompson

Printed in the United States of America

Published by:

The Leverage Factory, Inc.
1473 NW Lewis St.
Bend, OR 97701

www.leveragefactory.com
www.beawriter.US

ISBN: 0-9773000-1-3

10 9 8 7 6 5 4 3 2 1

DEDICATION

This book is dedicated to the two people who helped me be a
better writer. Dr. Tony Canedo, who passed away as I was finishing this book, taught me about the power of ideas through his
courses in the American novel at Central Washington Universit
Professor Harry Thomas, who I met while finishing up my
English degree at Boston University, introduced me to poetry
and encouraged me to strive for a natural voice in my writing.
Both of these talented, generous men gave me something most
students never get: their time. They both knew that the best
teaching is often done one-on-one long after class has ended.
I hope that I always live up to their standards of excellence in
education.

ABOUT THE AUTHORS

Steve Peha

Steve Peha is a leading voice on reading, writing, and education reform. As the founder of Teaching That Makes Sense, Inc. (TTMS), he has developed strategies that help teachers deliver more effective instruction and help kids improve their literacy skills.

TTMS provides education consulting, teacher training, and classroom modeling to school districts in the U.S. and Canada using the Reader's and Writer's Workshop method. In his materials, workshops, and books, Steve combines the best of classroom practice with a real-world, results-oriented perspective that makes teaching more practical for teachers and learning more meaningful kids.

Since founding TTMS in 1995, Steve has delivered hundreds of workshops for teachers, administrators, and parents. He has also addressed school boards, PTAs, and other organizations to discuss current challenges in education reform.

A trusted source for education journalists, he is widely quoted in the media discussing everything from teacher pay and high-stakes testing to the Achievement Gap and No Child Left Behind. His comments and opinion pieces have appeared in USA Today, The Christian Science Monitor, The Atlanta Journal-Constitution, The Miami Herald, The Austin American-Statesman, and The Milwaukee Journal-Sentinel, as well as in School Reform News and District Administration magazines.

In 2001, Steve was asked by The Seattle Times to write *The Effective Learning Series*, a bi-weekly column on best practice teaching that won the Innovators in Education Award from the Newspaper Association of America. Over the years, he has contributed more than 200 columns to this program, most recently an 18-part series on life skills for high school students.

Steve holds a BA in English from Boston University. He lives in Charrboro, North Carolina, with his wife, Margot Carmichael Lester, and their dog, Ursa.

For more information on Steve, visit the Teaching That Makes Sense website at www.ttms.org.

Margot Carmichael Lester

Margot Carmichael Lester stays on top of two careers, plying her trade as a professional writer and also as a business consultant.

Margot's writing appears regularly in magazines and newspapers as well as on the web. Her business journalism has been featured in Money Magazine, Multifamily Executive Magazine, The Los Angeles Business Journal, The Los Angeles Downtown News, The Triangle Business Journal and the Raleigh (N.C.) News & Observer. She is the author of *The Real Life Guide to Life After College* and *The Real Life Guide to Starting Your Career*. Her career advice appears monthly on Monster.com and in newspaper and magazine stories nationally.

Margot is also a love advice columnist, writing weekly for Match.com and MSN. In this capacity, she is frequently quoted as a relationship expert in publications around the country and on local, regional, and internet radio stations.

Prior to founding The Word Factory, her writing and consulting business, Margot served as director of marketing for the nationally-ranked Kenan-Flagler Business School at the University of North Carolina at Chapel Hill.

Margot began her writing career in high school as the school page columnist for her hometown paper, The Chapel Hill (N.C.) News.

Margot holds a BA in Journalism from The University of North Carolina at Chapel Hill. She lives in Carrboro, North Carolina, with her husband, Steve Peha, and their dog, Ursa.

For more information on Margot, visit her website at www.margotlester.com.

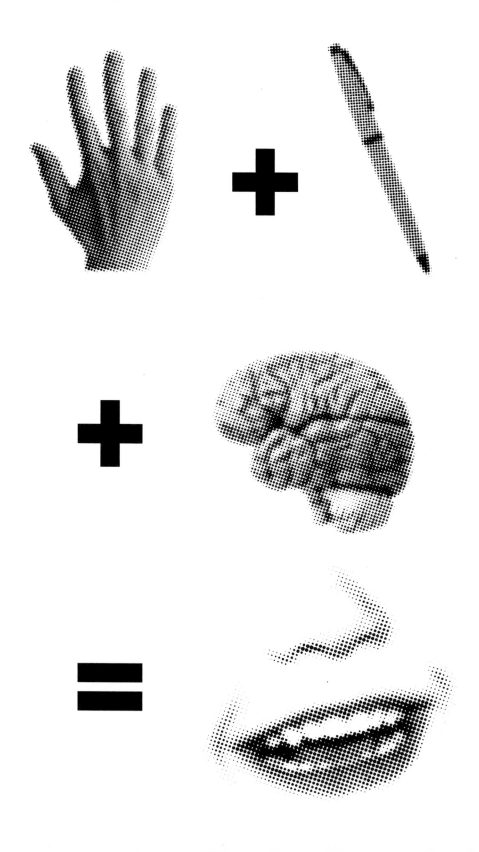

TABLE OF CONTENTS

CHAPTER 1: *Be a Better Writer*

CHAPTER 2: *Better Topics*

CHAPTER 3: *Better Ideas*

CHAPTER 4: *Better Organization*

CHAPTER 5: *Better Voice*

CHAPTER 6: *Better Words*

CHAPTER 7: *Better Sentences*

CHAPTER 8: *Better Punctuation*

BE A WRITER LIKE

ACTIVITY INDEX

READ LIKE A WRITER

CHAPTER ONE

Be a Better Writer

TEN THINGS YOU NEED TO KNOW
EVEN IF YOU DON'T READ THIS CHAPTER

1. Almost everyone over the age of seven or eight in our society can write at least a little. Writing is a common and necessary skill.

2. There are three reasons your parents and teachers might have for wanting you to be a better writer: to help you get better grades, to help you get into a better college, and to help you get a better job.

3. Even if you have the same reasons that your parents and teachers do for wanting to be a better writer, it's important to have reasons of your own as well.

4. Becoming a better writer is hard. Most people don't get much better after they leave school, and some don't improve much even while they're in school.

5. Being a better writer can open up many interesting opportunities for you.

6. Young writers are publishing more and more writing these days— even full-length books.

7. To make good improvement, writers need time, choice, audience, purpose, feedback, and models of good writing.

8. Making sure you're getting enough of the things writers need will help you push through times when you seem to be stuck.

9. How you practice writing has a lot to do with what you want to learn and how badly you want to get better.

10. Writing is a practice in the same way that being a doctor or a lawyer is a practice. Writers are always trying to learn, grow, and get better at what they do.

WHY BE A BETTER WRITER?

If you're standing in a bookstore right now and you just picked this book off a shelf, you can perform a little thought experiment. Look around and ask yourself: What percentage of the people in this store can write? If you toss out the toddlers, you'll probably say it's close to one hundred percent.

If you're not reading this in a bookstore, you can make the same calculation for any group of people you know. And it'll probably come out the same way. Small children aside, just about everyone in our society can write at least a little. So why would anyone need to get better?

We could always start with the Three Standard Adult Reasons for improving your writing skills. These are the reasons that your parents or teachers might want you to be a better writer. You've probably heard them a million times before, because the Three Standard Adult Reasons for kids getting better at anything relating to their education are always the same:

3

1. You'll get better grades.
2. You'll get into a better college.
3. You'll get a better job.

Better grades. Better college. Better job. Three things that tend to make our lives better as we grow up. Three things that most parents and teachers want for most kids. Three things that require good writing ability.

Writing is a key that can unlock many doors and offer you many interesting choices. And interesting choices are what the people who care about you want you to have. But what do *you* want? After all, you're the one who has to do the work to improve. Why do *you* want to be a better writer?

In some ways, your goals may not be much different than those of your parents or teachers. You, too, may want better grades, a better shot at college, and a better job when you get out. But you may want other things as well, and I'm curious to know what those are.

The reason I ask is this: Becoming a better writer is hard. Most people go through their entire adult lives and write pretty much the same way on the day they retire as they did on the day they left school. And even in school, most students don't improve much after sixth or seventh grade. They may be able to write faster or longer, they may know a few more big words, but the quality of what they write doesn't change.

So what's in this for you? When you think about being a better writer, what does writing better look like?

ACTIVITY: GOAL SETTING

Take a minute to think about the goals you have for yourself as a writer. For example, if you worked hard and made improvements, what would you be able to do that you can't do now? How might your writing be different? How would you feel about yourself? Think of three or four things and jot them down. Put them on a sticky note and keep them by your computer. Write them in the front of your journal. Put them any place where you can see them when you do your work. Keeping your goals in sight will make you more likely to achieve them.

WHY I WANTED TO BE A BETTER WRITER

I can still remember the first time I wanted to be a better writer. And sure enough, it had to do with Standard Adult Reason #2, getting into college. I was applying to transfer from the small school where I started to the big one where I really wanted to go. And I *really* wanted to go there. But I had to write two essays for my admissions application.

The first college I attended had not required admissions essays. In fact, it required so little of me with regard to writing, I didn't have to take the required freshman and sophomore English classes. To make matters worse, I was a music major there. While I spent many hours writing music, I almost never wrote a sentence.

There I was, twenty years old, needing to write a couple of sharp essays to convince a big university I was worthy of being admitted, and I discovered I didn't write very well. Truth was, I wrote okay. I was able to complete a slightly confused and rambling first draft of any essay I was assigned, but that was about it. In reading over what I'd written, I could tell my pieces had problems. But I couldn't figure out how to fix them. I didn't know how to make my own writing better, or how to make myself a better writer in the process.

I spent weeks on my admissions application, fretting every moment about my essays, and was eventually accepted. Two years later I got my degree—in English no less, a subject where I had to write all the time. But struggling with those essays made it painfully clear to me that I needed to be a better writer. I wanted to be better, too, because I was beginning to see that writing well was the key to many interesting opportunities.

TIP:

When we're trying to get better at something, we often have to look outside ourselves for help from other people. Start thinking now about people you know who might be able to help you become a better writer.

Over the last twenty years, I can think of several other times in my life when I've wished I were a better writer. And even though the circumstances change, the motivation is always the same: there's something I want, and writing is a good way to get it.

I would imagine that your reasons for wanting to be a better writer are a little different than mine. I'm assuming, of course, that you're somewhat less than twenty years old and that college, whether you decide to go or not, is at least a few years away. If you're like most kids, you're probably not that concerned about your grades either. And I can't imagine you're doing any serious career planning right now. So if it's not grades, college, or a job, what is it?

ACTIVITY: IMAGINE YOUR LIFE AS A BETTER WRITER

If you became a better writer, how do you think your life would change? What opportunities do you think might be available to you? Do you think you would feel differently about yourself? Writing is a deeply personal activity. When we change how we write, we change ourselves a little, too. Think about what that change might be like for you.

SO WHY DO YOU WANT TO BE A BETTER WRITER?

Over the years, as kids have told me about why they want to become better writers, and reflected on their reasons for wanting to improve, I've noticed that a few ideas come up over and over again. Here are the most common ones:

- **To write a book.** I'm amazed by the number of kids who want to be better writers so they can write books. The cool thing is that many can actually do it as long as they're willing to put in the hundreds of hours it typically takes. More kids are publishing more writing of all kinds these days—articles, essays, blogs, even full-length novels.

- **To explore your creativity.** Writing is, literally, creative. You start with something that exists only in your mind and make it real on the printed page. For some of us, this might be fiction. For others, poetry or song. Regardless of the form, many kids just want to create something. And writing is the way they like to create best.

- **To express yourself.** Do you ever have important thoughts and feelings you want to share? Is it sometimes hard to put them into words? These are great reasons to become a better writer. For many kids, this is the real inspiration. It's so frustrating when you can't communicate with people in ways they understand.

- **To be more like someone you admire.** We may not think this is our reason for wanting to be a better writer, but it often is. Some of us admire authors because of the great books we've read. Some of us may know an author or two, or have someone in our family who writes. For me, it was a friend from school who wrote many plays and stories; I wanted to be a better writer so I could be more like him.

- **To be famous and make money.** It's natural to look in a bookstore and imagine that every person whose name you see on a cover is rich and famous. A few of them are. But most are not. Writing is a hard way to pursue fame and fortune. At the same time, I know I've dreamed of it. What writer hasn't? So while it's not the best reason for wanting to become a better writer, it's certainly one of the most human.

Miss Margot says

I wanted to be a better writer when I was a kid because it was the thing I was best at. I was, and still am, a terrible reader. I wasn't a good actor, and I was only an okay swimmer. But I could write really well. I was always trying to be a better writer so I could be really good at something—and to offset the bad grades I got in reading. Now I still want to be a better writer. Sometimes it's because my other writer friends do something cool that I want to do, too. Other times it's because I could get paid more. So it's okay to have many different reasons for wanting to be a better writer.

If none of the reasons I've suggested strikes you as being exactly right, don't despair. Every writer is different. Of course, the best reason of all is simply that you love to write. Getting better at something you love to do is a great reward, even if you have no other reason for doing it.

ACTIVITY: WHAT DO YOU WANT TO ACCOMPLISH?

Another way to look at becoming a better writer is to think of specific goals you'd be willing to set for yourself. For example, you might want to complete a certain number of pieces each month or write a certain number of words each day. Having tangible, measurable goals to achieve can be challenging, but it can also be a terrific motivator, especially if you put your goals on a sticky note and post them where you can see them every day.

WHAT EVERY WRITER NEEDS TO BE A BETTER WRITER

As I've said, becoming a better writer is very hard. But fortunately, bigger brains than yours or mine have been working on this problem for many years. Believe it or not, people have actually done research to determine what writers need to improve. Here are some of the most important things they've come up with:

- **Time.** It takes time to get better at anything, and it appears to take a lot of time to get better at writing. How much time does it take? Probably about an hour a day, at least five days a week, for several months or so. Time spent on school writing assignments may not be much help. The time you need to put in is time spent on writing where you choose your own topics and determine what you want to write about them.

TIP:

As a younger writer, I lacked the discipline to write every day. I still don't do a great job of it, but I'm getting better. I knew that getting good at writing took a lot of time, so I would bunch that time up all on one day. Instead of working an hour a day, six days a week, for example, I might work six hours on a Saturday. This was not the best use of my time. Most writers benefit from working for a while and then putting their work away. Coming back to a piece a day or two later helps us see it with new eyes. So try to write regularly, a little bit each day, rather than just once in a while for a long period of time.

- **Choice.** Like so many things in life, becoming a better writer means making better choices. But in order to make better choices, you have to have the power to choose. When you make all the choices about your writing, it is truly yours—you own it. Because you own it, you'll work harder to make it the best it can be. And from that hard work will come the improvement you're hoping for.

- **Purpose.** In order to get better, writers need real reasons for writing. Knowing *why* you're writing something not only helps you get it written, it helps you figure out when you're finished. If your writing doesn't have a purpose, chances are you won't know when you've accomplished it.

- **Audience.** Of all the things writers need, audience is one of the most important. I can barely even come up with a topic without imagining who my audience will be. To me, writing feels like talking to people on paper, so I find it helpful to know who those people are. As you work to become a better writer, keep your readers in mind. Think about what they want and how you can give it to them.

- **Feedback.** Feedback tells you what people think about your work. In order to improve, you need constructive feedback from your readers, whether they're friends, teachers, family members, or other writers just like you. It's hard to get better by ourselves because our judgment about the quality of what we do isn't always reliable. We have to know what other people think about our work, and we have to ask them for detailed explanations of their opinions.

- **Models.** To produce better writing, it's helpful to know what better writing looks like. That's where reading comes in. Every time you read, you look at a model of someone else's writing. When you come across something you like, stop for a minute and ask yourself why you like it. Then think about how you might be able to use the same techniques—but not the same words—in your own work.

Miss Margot says

For as long as I can remember, I've kept a "swipe file". It's a folder full of sentences, phrases, and whole stories I've really liked. If I get stuck when I'm writing, I'll read through this folder to try to jog my own creativity. To help students get inspired, we keep a huge folder on our computer of hundreds of samples from other young writers. We use these all the time when we're teaching because they make the best lessons.

Is it possible to get better without these things? Sure it is. Do you have to have all of them all the time? No. Then what's the point of this big long list? To give you choices.

The road to better writing is a rocky one. Sometimes you'll be moving along just fine; other times you won't be moving at all. The key to breaking through difficult situations is asking yourself, "What do I need to become a better writer that I'm not getting right now?" Maybe you need to put in more time. Maybe you need to have someone read your work and give you feedback. Maybe you need to do some wider reading to find the kind of writing you're trying to create.

The point of this list is to show you what to look for when you're looking for what you need. Writing can be a lonely way to go through life. By thinking about the things writers need, and by making sure you're getting at least some of them, you'll be able to keep yourself going when the going gets tough.

ACTIVITY: WHAT DO YOU DO WHEN THE GOING GETS TOUGH?

When we make up our minds to get better at something, we often start with the idea that each day we'll make a small amount of progress. Unfortunately, this isn't true. Some days we don't get anywhere at all. On other days we may even feel like we've gotten a bit worse. How do you react when this happens? What do you do to pull yourself out of a slump? Does it work? Do you need new strategies? The best strategy I've learned over the years is to ask someone for help. Getting support from someone else can make all the difference in the world.

READ LIKE A WRITER

There's one more thing you need as you begin your journey toward better writing. You need to learn to read like a writer. Sounds a little weird, doesn't it? Let me explain.

Normally, when we read, we work to understand what the writer is trying to say. We follow the sequence of events or the steps in a logical argument. We figure out the meanings of the words and try to determine which ideas are most important.

But when we read like a writer, we focus less on *what* is being said and more on *why* and *how* it's being said. Specifically, we look at techniques the author is using to get the message across and how those techniques affect our experience.

TIP:

Reading is not the only way to learn to write, but since we all read so much, it's probably the easiest way. Most successful writers will tell you they've learned a lot about writing from reading. Everything you read has something to teach you. When you read something bad, think of it as a lesson on what not to do. When you read something great, think of it as the best teacher you could ever have.

Under normal circumstances, if we're reading along in a novel, we might ask questions like these: What's going to happen next? What happened to that person from six chapters ago? Why does the main character keep doing such stupid things? These kinds of questions help us follow the story and understand its meaning.

But when we read like a writer, we ask different kinds of questions:

- Why did the writer use that word instead of another one?

- Why is there a comma here instead of a period?

- What kind of lead was that?

- Why did the writer switch from long sentences to short ones?

- Why is the writer giving us so much descriptive detail about this character?

To read like a writer is to try to get inside the mind behind the words, to go beyond *what* writers write with the hope of understanding *why* and *how* they write it. This is not easy. But it's extremely valuable, and it's a vital skill to develop if you want to be a better writer.

The best way to be a better writer is to study writers who are better than you are. Fortunately, you probably encounter some every day in the books you read. Every good book is a course in good writing. Every page is full of useful techniques you can borrow for your own work— as long as you know how to recognize them.

Of course, the real benefit of learning to read like a writer is learning to read your own writing this way. To be a better writer, you have to become aware of the choices you make when you write. You have to ask yourself the same questions you ask of other writers you read: Why did I use this word instead of that one? Would it still make sense if I took out this sentence? Which of these three leads works best?. We're not used to paying attention to ourselves in this way. Most of us just write, and then we read it over again to make sure it sounds okay. But that's just writing. What you want is better writing.

Read Like a Writer:

Why Ask Why?

The next time you pick up a book, look for things in the writing you can ask writerly questions about. "Why" questions are usually best. Ask yourself, "Why did the chapter start this way? Why did the writer use that word? Why don't we know more about this character yet?" Even if you don't come up with the answers, asking the questions will put you on the path to reading more like a writer.

Learning to read like a writer takes time and practice. So don't be too hard on yourself if it doesn't make sense right away. Throughout this book you'll find many things to help you. Over time you'll improve. And best of all, your writing will improve, too.

ACTIVITY: START A "FAVORITE PASSAGES" JOURNAL

Occasionally, as you're reading, you'll find a small part of a story or article you really like. When this happens, write it down (or type it up if you're working on a computer). Start collecting examples of your favorite passages from things you read. All you have to do is copy down the words (usually just a few sentences or a few short paragraphs at most) and add a line or two about why you like it. After a while, you'll start to see patterns in the passages you collect. Soon you'll be able to pattern your own writing after the best stuff you've collected.

PRACTICE MAKES...

Perfect. If you've heard it once, you've heard it a thousand times. Practice makes perfect, right? Wrong. Practice doesn't make perfect. Practice makes permanent.

Think about it for a second. Let's say I recommend a technique and you practice it wrong 100 times. What have you learned? The wrong way to do something. All that practicing didn't make a good technique perfect; it made a bad technique permanent because of the way you practiced it. Practice only makes perfect if you practice perfectly.

No one practices perfectly. But we can all aspire to perfection. So here are a few tips to improve the way you practice the techniques in this book:

- **Work on real pieces of writing.** To make real progress, you need to do real work. It might seem easiest to make up meaningless pieces and see if the techniques I suggest are helpful. There's nothing wrong with this, but I think you'll get more out of my advice if you apply it to real pieces you really care about.

- **Try it several different ways.** In most cases, I will only show you how to do something one particular way. But you should try it as many different ways as you can. My way may not be the best way for you. Experimenting with a different way of doing something is not the same as practicing it wrong because you're aware of what you're doing.

- **Make conscious comparisons.** Don't just use a technique and decide casually that it makes your writing better or worse. Look closely at your writing before and after to see how the quality changes. Some techniques don't work well for every writer in every situation. The question to ask isn't "Do I like this technique?" it's "Does this technique make my writing better?"

TIP:

Though most people hate doing it, writing something several different ways is a great way to improve. The English language has almost 500,000 words—three to four times more than most other languages. For any sentence or paragraph you write, there are almost always other ways to say the same thing. Exploring these ways, and learning which ones work best for you, is probably the most important practice you can undertake.

- **Watch out for side effects.** Even if you find a technique you like, don't use it too much. Strange things happen when you rely too heavily on certain strategies—worst case, your reader will get bored. Ultimately, you don't want to write with a bunch of techniques you learned from a book. You want to make those techniques a part of who you are as a writer so they become natural parts of the way you write.

- **Make it your own.** The best thing you can do is develop your own writing techniques. An easy way to do this is to base them on techniques you learn from others. Writing is very personal, and the techniques writers use are personal, too. Just as you make choices about *what* you write, you need to make choices about *how* you write as well.

Miss Margot says

I never thought much about my writing technique until I met Mr. Peha. Then I realized I had devised a couple of tricks to write good leads (that's what journalists call the opening of a story), and another one to write good nut grafs (that's what journalists call the paragraph that tells what the story is all about). So you might actually be developing your own techniques already and just not know it!

Writing takes practice. But not exactly the kind of practice you have for football or soccer or some other sport. In sports, there's a difference between practice and play. But in the practice of writing, it's always game time. Writers practice their art in the same way doctors practice medicine and lawyers practice law. These professionals are always doing real work even though they are also always practicing.

To practice writing, in this sense, means that no matter how good we get, we're always trying to improve—or figure out why we're not improving. And that, of course, is the spirit of this book. With every piece we write, and every technique we try, we're always working to become better writers.

BE A WRITER LIKE LARRY L. COX

Larry L. Cox writes marketing materials for an insurance company to help agents sell life insurance products and to help consumers understand them. He's also the author of On the Waters: Fishing for Life's Simple Pleasures *and* Close Encounters of the Loon Kind. *In his past, he has been a juvenile delinquent, a university student in Europe, a high school English teacher in the Bahamas, a clothing salesman, a life insurance agent, a son, a brother, a husband, a father, and a grandfather.*

Q WHAT KIND OF WRITER ARE YOU?

A I'm a versatile writer; I write pretty well in a variety of forms and styles. On the literary side, I have on occasion written poems, short stories, essays, feature articles, technical articles, a textbook chapter, a memoir book, and a nature book. In the business world, I've written advertising, annual reports, how-to sales articles, motivational talks, presidential speeches, and product marketing materials. Each of these requires a different set of skills.

I love words. I believe that's where it all begins. As a wild young man, I never felt I was ever really listened to or understood, so I now feel compelled to turn my words into beautiful pieces. I want people to listen to me and to learn from my unique take on the world.

Q WHY DO YOU WRITE?

A I started writing as a means to impress rather than to express! That was stupid. Always write to express your ideas as clearly and succinctly as you can. It took me a long time to learn to write clearly, concisely, and persuasively. But that is the goal of all writing (and speaking, too, by the way). The objective must be, first and foremost, to be read. Nothing happens until a piece of writing connects with a reader.

But just as reading opens up a world of infinite possibilities to you, so does writing. You are unique in how you think and feel and experience the world. If you are willing to discipline yourself to learn the craft of writing, you can change people's lives through words. If you're reading this, are affected by it, and are inspired to write yourself, then I'm changing your life! Pass it on.

Q

WHAT MADE YOU WANT TO BE A WRITER?

A

I admired—and truthfully was a bit in awe of—a high school buddy, Mike Oiseth. Mike introduced me to classical music, fine films, great art, and also great literature. But I spent many of my high school years getting into trouble—with teachers for being disruptive and with the police for minor but stupid offenses. Finally, a month before I was to graduate from high school, I was thrown out for punching a teacher. I was actually attending my fifth year of high school when I met Mike! By then I was starting to wise up and grow up because I wanted desperately to go to college and to do something with my life other than earning minimum wage slinging burgers. After hanging out with Mike for a while, I started writing stories. He encouraged me, even though they were terrible at first, and little by little they got better.

WHAT ADVICE WOULD YOU GIVE TO A FELLOW WRITER WHO WAS JUST STARTING OUT?

1. Take risks.

2. Read, read, read.

3. Learn how to write different things in different styles.

4. Gather up the gumption to ask a teacher for extra help in writing.

5. To get good, be willing to revise, revise, and revise your work some more.

6. Keep a journal and write like crazy!

7. Never let someone kill your dream.

8. Remember these three key words: inform, instruct, inspire.

9. Remember what Nathaniel Hawthorne said: "Easy reading is darn hard writing."

Get to it! The world is waiting to know your work.

BE A BETTER WRITER

CHAPTER TWO

Better Topics

TEN THINGS YOU NEED TO KNOW
EVEN IF YOU DON'T READ THIS CHAPTER

1. It can be hard to write when someone picks your topics for you. It can also be hard to come up with good topics on your own.

2. To come up with good topics consistently, use topic selection strategies to help you find ideas that will inspire you to write well.

3. Rather than trying to pick a new topic every time you sit down to write, it's better if you make lists of potential topics ahead of time.

4. Your own life experiences are the best source of writing topics you will ever discover.

5. Even typical everyday experiences can make great topics if you think about them in different ways.

6. The best writing topics are those you have strong feelings about, especially if you have both positive and negative feelings about them.

7. Always make sure the topics you pick to write about are appropriate. If you're not sure, check with your parents, your teachers, or another adult.

8. Sometimes, especially in school, you don't get to choose your topic. But even in these situations, there are still ways to come up with something you can get excited about.

9. When you have a research project in a subject area like Social Studies or Science, you can often find a good topic by looking for connections between the subject you are studying and the things you are interested in.

10. After you have worked out several lists of possible topics for yourself, you can begin to see patterns that will help you find the right things to write about every time.

IN SEARCH OF INSPIRING TOPICS

When I was a kid, I hated to write. I never did it at home on my own, and even in school I'd complain when my teachers assigned it. When I absolutely had to write, my goal was always to produce the minimum amount so I could get done as quickly as possible.

Looking back, I'm not sure what my problem was. Writing wasn't that hard for me. It just seemed like a stupid thing to do. I think what I reacted most negatively to were the topics my teachers told me to write about. I never liked having someone else pick my topic for me. At the same time, however, I refused to come up with topics of my own. My teachers were probably as frustrated with me as I was with writing.

Because topic selection was such a hard thing for me when I was a student, I've thought a lot about it as a teacher. What I've concluded is this: when it comes to topic selection, most of us need something in between having someone pick topics for us and having to pick our own topics out of thin air.

TIP:

Don't discount the importance of finding just the right topic. I've seen dramatic differences in the quality of writing kids produce when they write about things they really care about. It's more than just having a lot to say; it's being inspired to say it and having that inspiration come through in the quality of your voice and your use of language.

Most of us struggle, at least a little, when someone else tells us what to write about. We may not care about the topic or know much about it. At the same time, we may not be inspired to come up with an inspiring topic on our own. And then we're stuck: no topic, no ideas about the topic, no words to express those ideas, no writing.

The best approach is to look for a middle way, something in between having your topics given to you and having to come up with them entirely on your own. As a teacher trying to help students come up with good topics, I've developed a set of topic selection strategies. These simple list-building activities don't tell you what topics to pick. Instead they tell you how to pick topics that often inspire good writing.

Miss Margot says

As a professional writer, I get to pick my topic only sometimes. When I do, it's great because I get to research stuff I'm interested in and write big stories about it. But other times, editors, just like teachers, tell me what stories to write. I've learned to make those fun by getting into learning about a new subject. For example, I never thought real estate was very interesting until I was assigned to write a story on it. Now I write about it all the time and I love it. There's almost always something interesting about a story. The trick is being open to finding it.

Ideally, we would all like to have a big collection of good topics to choose from, so that whenever we sat down to write, we'd be ready to go. But that won't happen if we're always coming up with topics one at a time. What we need to do is create several lists and see what shows up on them. With luck we'll find ourselves inspired by many things.

THE TYPICAL-UNUSUAL T-CHART

The first rule of writing is "Write what you know." And what you know best is your own life. Your life experience is the greatest list of topics you'll ever run across. But how do you make a list of everything that has ever happened to you?

You don't.

A better approach is to use the Typical-Unusual T-Chart. In this topic selection strategy, we list typical, everyday life experiences on one side and unusual, once-in-a-lifetime experiences on the other.

TYPICAL	UNUSUAL
Getting up in the morning	Visited the famous Biltmore Estate
Walking the dog	Went to Paris for my honeymoon
Visiting schools	Got married in a bowling alley
Having a Coke after lunch to keep myself awake	Won $75 in a chess tournament when I was 12
Grocery shopping	Went to London
E-mail	Smashed my car into a bus
Writing	Performed on stage with Bill Gates
Reading	Got stuck in an old building during an earthquake
Playing music	
Getting lost	

These lists can go on and on, of course. Some people come up with twenty or more items on each side. It might take a few minutes to get started, so don't worry if things go slowly at first.

WRITING FROM THE TYPICAL SIDE

At first glance, it might be hard to see how topics on the "Typical" side of the chart would be worth writing about. But the theory is this: because you do the things on the typical side all the time, you know a lot about them and therefore may have many interesting things to say.

Take the first item, for example. "Getting up in the morning" might not seem like a good topic. But if I think about it for a minute, several interesting ideas emerge. Obviously, I've been getting up in the morning all my life. But the truth is, I hate it. I've always had trouble getting out of bed, especially when it's cold and dark. Sometimes, if I wake up early in the middle of the winter, I'll stay hidden under the covers listening to the radio for hours. I've often wondered why something as normal as getting out of bed every morning could be so challenging. I've tried everything I can to make things better. Nothing seems to work. And it doesn't matter how early I go to sleep the night before.

Are you beginning to see the possibilities? There might be half a dozen good ideas here. Within something as simple as getting up in the morning, I may have interesting thoughts, strong feelings, personal insights, even stories to tell. Who knows what I could do with this topic or any of the others on the "Typical" side?

ACTIVITY: DRILL DOWN INTO THE TYPICAL

We tend to discount the typical things in our lives because they don't seem very interesting to us. But we can often get to more interesting things if we drill down a bit to get more specific. For example, a typical thing in my life is watching TV. But if I drill down one level, I can come up with better topics like watching NFL football, watching Star Trek, or watching DVD movies on Friday nights with my wife. Now I have a few more interesting things to write about. So how about you? Take two or three things from the "Typical" side and drill down into them to see what better topics you can come up with.

WRITING FROM THE UNUSUAL SIDE

Topics from the "Unusual" side of the chart seem like natural ones to write about. After all, these are unique or otherwise special experiences that stand out well enough for you to remember them even years later. These are the big moments in your life, the highlights, the stories you tell over and over.

Writing these stories down is a way to preserve them and to share them with others. We're all fascinated by the unusual things that happen to people we know. And even when we don't know the people involved, we still love hearing stories that are out of the ordinary or different from our own lives.

ACTIVITY: THE TIME WHEN...

If you're having trouble coming up with things for the "Unusual" side, there's another way that works better for some writers. I call it "The time when...". Instead of thinking, "What's an unusual thing that has happened to me?" think of a time when something happened. For example, in my life, I could think of the time when I fell and hit my head, or the time when I rode a train across Europe, or the time when I almost pitched a no-hitter. How about you?

THE LIKE-HATE T-CHART

Good topics come from strong feelings. And strong feelings come from the things we like and the things we hate.

In this topic selection strategy, we list things we like on one side of a T-chart and things we hate on the other. (When I'm teaching in school, I make a rule that we don't put people on the "Hate" side. Even when we're not in school, this is still a good rule.)

LIKE	HATE
Reading	Driving
Watching NFL football	Cold weather
Teaching	Teaching
Our dog	Cleaning my office
Pizza	Exercising
Hanging out with friends	Going to the dentist
Playing Scrabble	Fixing things when they break
Computers	Running errands
Fishing	Watching nature shows

As with the Typical-Unusual lists, we might be able to go on forever here. And everything we put down is likely to be a good topic because it will be charged with emotion.

WRITING FROM THE LIKE-HATE T-CHART

Our pieces can take many different shapes when we write from topics on the Like-Hate T-Chart. We can talk about why we like or hate a particular thing. We can talk about how we came to feel the way we do. Or we can write up a story that really happened in our lives. We can even combine all three approaches.

BOTH SIDES NOW

When I teach this strategy in school, students often ask if they can put the same topic down on both sides. The answer is yes. In fact, I encourage you to find things you can legitimately put on both sides because this means you have two sets of strong feelings about something.

In my example, I listed "Teaching" on both sides. Some days, when it's going well, I love teaching. There's almost no better feeling in the world than helping people learn. But there are many days when no one seems to be learning. These are the days when the kids are hard to work with, or when I'm very tired, or when I don't know what to do. On these days, teaching is just too hard, and I absolutely hate it.

Having these kinds of conflicting feelings about something usually makes a piece better. People will definitely want to know why you feel the way you do. But they'll also want to know how you deal with liking and hating something at the same time. This is the stuff of great writing.

ACTIVITY: PLAY THE "WHY" GAME

Sometimes, topics on the Like-Hate T-Chart don't seem to go anywhere. But you can make them go somewhere by playing the "Why" game. For example, if I say I like computers, you could ask me why. I'd say because they help me create cool things. And you could ask me why that's important. And I'd say because creating things is how I make a contribution to the world. Now I've developed a set of connections to my original topic that might help me create a more interesting piece. You can play the "Why" game by yourself, but it's more fun, and probably a little easier, if someone plays with you.

THE FUN-HAVE TO T-CHART

Everybody loves to have fun. In fact, I'll bet many of us wish we could have fun all the time. But we can't because there's always something we have to deal with that isn't fun, something we have to do just because it has to be done.

You may find that this topic selection strategy produces results similar to the Like-Hate T-Chart. That's okay. I often find that using this strategy helps me come up with at least a few things I hadn't thought of before.

FUN	HAVE TO DO
Sleeping in late	Cleaning the bathroom
Watching TV with lots of snacks	Raking the leaves
Traveling by car	Watching what I eat
Playing chess	Driving
Going out to dinner	Figuring out my taxes
Spending a few days at the beach	Going to the doctor
Getting new DVDs from NetFlix	Getting my car fixed
	Keeping my office clean
	Feeding the dog

All of these topics could probably appear on the Like-Hate T-Chart. But when I think of them in the context of things I do for fun versus things I do because I have to, different ideas occur to me. For example, because I enjoy playing chess, it seems interesting to think about why it's so much fun. It's a game I've liked since I was a kid. I also enjoy reading about it. I don't even get to play it very much as an adult, but I still think it's fun. Why?

Then again, topics on the "Have To" side give me a look at parts of my life I don't think about much. For example, my wife and I just bought a house and the trees in our yard drop thousands of leaves in the fall. It's up to us to rake them; nobody else is going to do it. Last weekend, we spent several hours raking. It's not something we would ever do if we didn't have to. On the other hand, having to do it wasn't the end of the world. It was nice doing it together and when it was finished, I felt good that we had cleaned up the yard. So even though this was something I had to do, it wasn't a bad experience. It's things like this that make good topics for writing.

ACTIVITY: ARE THINGS ON THE HAVE-TO SIDE REALLY SO BAD?

When I look at the Fun-Have To T-Chart, I almost always pick something off the "Have To" side. I just seem to get more interesting pieces this way. What I've discovered is that exploring the things I have to do in my life generates interesting ideas for writing, especially when I consider that many of these things have a positive side to them. So take a look at what you've got on the "Have To" side of your chart and ask yourself, "What's good about this?" It might lead you to some interesting work.

THE PROUD OF-REGRET T-CHART

We've all had moments in our lives when we felt proud. Maybe we were proud of ourselves for reaching a certain goal. Or maybe we were proud of someone in our family or a close friend. We've also had moments of regret. Perhaps we did something wrong. Or maybe we let an important opportunity go by without doing anything about it.

Pride and regret are two of the strongest feelings we can have. And because of that, the Proud Of-Regret T-Chart makes a good topic selection strategy.

PROUD OF	REGRET
Having a good marriage	Breaking a window when I was little playing baseball in the house
My house	
The books I've written	Staying late at a party and lying to my mom about it
The software products I've developed	
The record album I made in college	Not practicing my music more when I was in high school and college
The award I won from the Newspaper Association of America	Not studying French more in high school when I was getting really good at it

The pieces you write from these lists will often turn out to be similar to those on the "Unusual" side of the Typical-Unusual T-Chart. Most people don't come up with as many topics on these lists as they do on the others. But often the topics they do come up with are better ones.

The topics that come up on this chart are sometimes more serious than the topics that come up on the other charts. You have to decide if that's okay. You may want to talk to your parents, to your or teachers, or to other adults to figure out what's appropriate.

Writing about serious things from our lives can sometimes be good. But at other times, it isn't appropriate. It can also be hard to write about serious things. There are topics from my own life that I've tried to write about several times and never made much progress with.

When it comes to choosing your own topics, you always have to ask yourself if what you choose is something you should be writing about. The answer isn't always clear. Sometimes you just have a feeling. Sometimes you have to ask someone. Sometimes you're not sure until you start writing—or even until you finish.

ACTIVITY: GO BEYOND YOURSELF

When we fill out the Proud Of-Regret T-Chart, it's natural to think of ourselves first. As a result, we fill the chart with things we take personal pride in and things we regret about our own life experience. But we don't have to stop there. We can take pride in our family, our school, our community, anything in the world we feel some connection to. The same is true for regrets. For example, many people regret the damage our society does to the environment. See if you can go beyond yourself in this way. You might come up with even better topics you feel strongly about.

BE A WRITER LIKE G. D. GEARINO

G. D. Gearino is the author of What the Deaf-Mute Heard, *a novel that was later made into a Hallmark Hall of Fame movie that received three Emmy nominations. His second book,* Counting Coup, *was published in July 1997, and a third novel,* Blue Hole, *was published in August 1999. He's also a weekly columnist for the Raleigh, N.C., News & Observer, where he once served as the business editor. Prior to that, he worked as a reporter, editor, and columnist at newspapers in Florida, Colorado, Wyoming, Michigan, Montana, and Alberta, Canada.*

Q WHAT KIND OF WRITER ARE YOU?

I'm both a writer of journalism and a writer of novels. I was a reporter and columnist for many years before dabbling in fiction (or more precisely, before being open about my fiction). But mostly, I'm the kind of writer that likes to get paid for writing.

Q WHY DO YOU WRITE?

See above. I have no marketable skills, yet I have a deep aversion to hard work. A man's got to make a living somehow.

Q

A

WHAT MADE YOU WANT TO BE A WRITER?

The fear of having to spend my adult life working as an accountant, which is what my father was. Also, the five months I labored as a heavy equipment operator in Wyoming (a job I took after quitting a perfectly good newspaper job in a snit). That five months of real work showed me what a sweet gig the writing life can be. You work inside, you don't get dirty, and people love it when you casually say, "Well, I'm a writer."

Q

A

WHAT ADVICE WOULD YOU GIVE TO A FELLOW WRITER WHO WAS JUST STARTING OUT?

Write something every day. A dancer dances. A mechanic fixes engines. A firefighter puts out fires. If you're not writing every day, you're not a writer, you're a hobbyist.

TOPIC CHOICE WHEN THERE IS NO CHOICE

When you're writing at home on your own, you get to choose the topics you write about. But when you're at school, topics are sometimes chosen for you. This is common in subjects like Social Studies and Science where your teachers have a curriculum they're required to cover and you're required to learn. When you have to do a research report or any informational writing project, you may have to work in a topic area you don't care about or even know about. How do you deal with that?

When it comes to research reports, most of us find ourselves at a disadvantage right from the start because we try to tackle unworkable topics. This happened to me in seventh grade. My Social Studies teacher told each of us to pick a different country and write a report on it. Because we knew little about our subjects, and because our teacher's requirements were so broad, most of us just copied or paraphrased information from encyclopedias. There really wasn't much else we could do, given how little we knew about our topics and how we were supposed to research them.

So what will you do the next time you're asked to do a research project on something you don't know much about or don't have much interest in? You'll have to get creative and try to find meaningful connections between the things your teachers want you to study and the things you know from your own life.

Miss Margot says

One way I avoid taking on topics that won't work is to write a pitch. A pitch is a short overview (150 words at most) of the story I'm proposing. It has a quick summary of the article, a list of important things I'll be writing about, and a brief discussion of why readers will care about it. To write a pitch, I usually have to do a little research but not very much. And my editor gets an idea of where the story's going or why it might be good before she assigns it. It works for everyone. It might even work for you and your teachers!

TOPIC EQUATIONS

The best research is always done by researchers who are passionate about their topics. This passion typically comes from a strong personal connection between the researcher and the topic being researched. We can think of that connection in terms of a mathematical equation:

Area of Interest + Area of Study = Possible Research Topic.

The first thing to do is make lists of things you're interested in. The lists I use most often include: "Things I Like," "Things I Do For Fun," "Things I Care About," and "Things I'm Interested In". You can make up your own lists if you like, but these work well for me and for many of the students I work with.

Here's a great set of lists one student came up with:

LIKE	FUN
Money	Play baseball
Rap music	Take trips
Clothes	Go to the mall
Pizza	Hang out with friends
Video games	Surf the Internet
Movies	Talk on the phone

CARE ABOUT	INTERESTED IN
My family	Getting a part-time job
My pets	Computers
My friends	Cars
Violence in my community	Going to college
People being treated fairly	

Once you have your lists, the trick is to find connections between certain items and the subject area you are studying. For example, if one of the things you like is the TV show Star Trek, and you're studying 20th Century U.S. History, then doing research on the space program might be perfect for you. If you're studying ancient Rome, however, you might not be able to make such an easy connection with that topic, so you'll have to think about it in a different way or pick another item on your list and try to make a different connection.

Here's how that same student used his lists and the Topic Equation strategy to come up with possible topics for his report on the Civil War:

INTEREST	SUBJECT	TOPICS
Baseball	The Civil War	Sports during the period Baseball's history as a popular pastime
Money	The Civil War	Standard of living Purchasing power of the average family Types of coin and paper money Raising money for the war effort
Part-time Job	The Civil War	Work opportunities for young people Wages and availability of work The impact of slavery on jobs in undeclared border states
Family	The Civil War	Family structure and relationships North-South cultural traditions Roles and expectations Families with relatives on both sides
Rap Music	The Civil War	Popular music of the period Political songs and poems
Community Violence	The Civil War	Safety of urban areas Crime rates Police work Lincoln's assassination

It's not easy to pick research topics in traditional school subject areas using the Topic Equation approach. It takes some time, some thought, some creativity, and even a little luck. But the effort is worthwhile. When you work with a topic that is well-defined and well-connected to something you understand and care about, you have more fun, your learning increases, and you do better work.

Miss Margot says

Did you know there are people who work at magazines and newspapers whose whole job is research? They check facts and gather information for reporters and other writers on staff. It's a very important job. And even though every researcher might not be passionate about every topic they have to work on, they are passionate about finding answers.

ACTIVITY: MAKE YOUR OWN TOPIC EQUATIONS

You can use the Topic Equation strategy even when you're not studying a subject in school. Just put any two general topics togeher and see what associations come up. For example, you could take baseball, put it together with rock music, and get topics like songs that refer to baseball, baseball players who are musicians, or the importance of music in sports (especially televised sports). You won't always be able to come up with something, but every once in a while you'll get a fabulous idea that wouldn't have occurred to you any other way.

YOUR TOPIC TERRITORIES

In some ways, it's so much harder being a kid than it is being an adult. Take writing, for example. As a kid in school, you have to be able to write about many different topics with new ones coming at you in every subject every year. Most adult professional writers, however, only have to write about the one topic they know best. This is their territory, the topic area where they do their best work, and where they feel the most comfortable.

Read Like a Writer:

Understanding Territories

How do professional writers explore their territories? Take some time to look at newspapers and magazines focusing on stories in subjects that interest you. Find a few authors who seem to write regularly about the same topics. Begin to associate writers with their territories. Then ask yourself, "How do these writers continue to come up with new ideas in the same old topics?"

Part of learning how to select the best topics is knowing which topics are best for you. In school, your teachers may not want you to come back to the same topics again and again. But in real life, this is exactly what most writers do. Of course, they don't continue to say the same things about the same topics—that would be boring. But many professional writers stake out their territories in the world of ideas and spend most of their careers exploring as much of them as they can.

Miss Margot says

When journalists write about one area regularly, it's called covering a beat. I've covered several different beats over the years. Right now, I mostly cover the commercial real estate and personal relationships beats—two very different topics. There are also people called general assignment reporters who cover anything that comes up—a big accident one day, a business story the next. They don't get to learn one thing really well (except writing), but they learn a lot of things pretty well.

You need to stake out your topic territories, too. You need to figure out the topics you like best—the ones that inspire you to do your best writing. But how can you do that without writing for years and years? Your topic T-charts may give you a clue.

Let's say you filled out all four charts in this chapter and that you averaged ten topics on each side of each chart. That's a total of eighty different topics. But they won't all be different. In some cases, similar topics may show up on different charts. This might indicate a promising territory.

Some of your best pieces may come from combining ideas. For example, on the "Proud Of" side of my Proud Of–Regret T-Chart, I listed the books I've written, the software products I've developed, and the record album I made in college. Maybe I could write about creating things and why that's so important to me.

The point is to keep using your lists as tools long after you make them. Go back and add new things. Look across several lists to find patterns. Take them out any time you need inspiration. Eventually, you may not need them at all. After a while, you'll know the topic territories you like best. Then your task will be to spend the rest of your life exploring them.

 YOUR CHECKLIST FOR BETTER TOPICS

Just because it comes off a good list doesn't mean it's a good topic. Think about some of the topics you've picked and see how they stack up against the criteria below.

A good topic is:

Something you have strong feelings about. What are those feelings? How will you communicate those feelings to your reader? Is there a key moment or a particularly important detail you want to emphasize so your reader will understand exactly how you feel?

_____

Something you know a lot about. What are the main things you want to cover? What's the most important part of your piece? What's the one most important thing you want your audience to know about your topic?

_____

Something you can describe in great detail. What are some of the details of your topic? Why are these details important? How do these details help the reader understand your message?

_____

Something your audience will be interested in. Who is your audience? Why will they be interested in your topic? What will interest them most?

_____

Something your audience will feel was worth reading. What will your audience gain from reading your piece? Will your audience learn something new? What will make your audience want to follow your piece all the way to the end?

_____

Every topic you pick does not have to meet every one of these requirements. In fact, all you really need to get started are the first two. The other three are important, but you may not know how to work with them until you've finished your first draft.

CHAPTER THREE

Better Ideas

TEN THINGS YOU NEED TO KNOW
EVEN IF YOU DON'T READ THIS CHAPTER

1. Topics and ideas are not the same thing. Topics are the things you write about; ideas are the things you write about them.

2. The main idea of a piece of writing is the one most important thing the writer wants the reader to know.

3. The first place to look for details is in the mind of the reader. Try to anticipate your readers' questions, and add details based on what you think they want to know.

4. The Idea-Details strategy makes adding details to a piece of writing easy.

5. Another easy way to add details is to think of categories like actions, feelings, thoughts, dialog, and so on.

6. Descriptive or "showing" details help readers get a clearer picture of what you're writing about.

7. You can sometimes improve your "showing" details if you close your eyes and visualize the scene you're writing about.

8. To determine the purpose of a piece of writing, ask "Why did the writer write this?"

9. Having a clear purpose in mind when you write will help you become a better writer because you'll be more conscious of what you're trying to achieve.

10. The key to coming up with ideas that are both original and popular is to be just different enough to get your readers' attention, but not so different that they can't relate to you.

A GAME OF IDEAS

In the previous chapter, we talked about better topics, so why in this chapter are we talking about better ideas? Because they're not the same thing. Topics are the things you write about; ideas are the things you write about them. If that sounds confusing, don't worry. This chapter will help you sort it out.

Writing is full of problems. The first problem we have to solve is what to write about. That's where choosing a topic comes in. But as soon as we have that one out of the way, we face an even tougher challenge. Now that we have something to write about, what are we going to write about it? What ideas are we going to express in our piece?

When we're sitting in front of a blank page or staring at an empty computer screen, we tend to think our problem is that we don't have any ideas in mind. But often it's just the reverse—we have too many ideas swimming around inside our head. For any topic we might choose, there's an almost infinite range of things we might choose to say about it. And while being a writer involves putting ideas on paper, being a better writer is involves knowing which ideas are better than others.

When we look at the ideas in a piece of writing, there are five things to think about:

- **An important main idea.** When our readers finish reading a piece of our writing, they should be able to figure out our message, the one most important thing we want them to know. It's as if we could scrunch the entire piece down to a single sentence and tell our readers that this one thing is what it's really all about.

- **Interesting details.** Details are the key to creating writing that holds a reader's interest. With every idea you put into a piece, readers become more curious. By including the right details, you answer their questions, satisfy their curiosity, and provide an enjoyable reading experience.

- **Showing, not just telling.** Readers are blind. Yes, they can see the words on the page, but they can't really see what's happening in the piece unless the writer shows them with descriptive language. I can write that the weather is awful, but you won't know what it's like outside my window unless I show you with words that make pictures in your mind.

- **A clear and meaningful purpose.** Good writers have good reasons for writing the things they do. But do those reasons come through when we read? As we decide which ideas to include in a piece, we always want to think about why we chose to write it in the first place.

- **Something surprising or unusual that works.** Many writers choose the same topics. For example, just about everyone has written about a pet, a vacation, or a bad thing that happened. So our challenge is to include ideas that make the telling of these stories different in ways our readers will enjoy.

Ultimately, writing is a game of ideas. Being a better writer means learning to play this game more effectively. To increase our effectiveness, we improve our understanding of the five elements that shape our ideas. Then we learn strategies to manipulate those elements, which is what we'll be doing in the rest of this chapter.

 YOUR CHECKLIST FOR BETTER IDEAS

You can be a better writer by developing your ideas more effectively. Take a piece you've written and see if it has the following elements. If it doesn't, use this checklist as a guide for revision.

A piece of writing with good ideas has:

An important main idea. What's the one most important thing you want your reader to know? Why is it important to you? Why is it important to your reader? How will your reader figure out what it is?

Interesting details. Which details are the most interesting? How do they help your reader understand your main idea? Have you answered your reader's most important questions?

Showing, not just telling. Where do you use showing details? How does the showing help to improve the reader's understanding? Can the reader see what's happening?

A clear and meaningful purpose. Why did you write this? Why is this a good reason to write something? When your readers have finished your piece, what do you want them to think and/or do?

Something surprising or unusual that works. What is surprising or unusual about your piece? What have you included that might be different from other things your readers have read about the same topic?

Of these five elements, an important main idea and interesting details are the most crucial to a successful piece. By working on just these two things you can often improve the other three at the same time.

THE ONE MOST IMPORTANT THING

Everybody loves going on vacation. And everyone seems to love writing about vacations, too. Over the years, I've read hundreds of pieces from students about their vacations. It's a good topic, one that often shows up on the "Unusual" side of their Typical-Unusual T-Charts. But even though vacations are great things to write about, the writing that emerges is often less than great. Many of the pieces sound like this:

> On the first day, we did this and this and this. Then, on the second day, we did this and this and this. Then we went here and then we went there and then on the last day we did this and this and this. And then we came home.

Most of these pieces are just lists of things that happened, sometimes dozens of things if the vacation was a long one. Even if the vacation was interesting, this kind of writing usually isn't. A list of details strung together one right after another is boring.

After I've read one of these pieces, I almost always ask the writer, "What's the one most important thing you want me to know?" At first, this seems like a hard question to answer. After all, the writer may think there isn't one most important thing, there may be a list of twenty things, and they all might seem equally important.

That's the problem. If the writer isn't sure about the one most important thing, the reader isn't sure either. And when readers can't figure out what's important, they don't know what to pay attention to. This is when they start to lose interest.

Read Like a Writer:

What's the Main Idea?

Whenever you read something, especially if it's something short like a newspaper article, magazine article, or web page, take a guess as to what you think the main idea is. Ask yourself, "What's the one most important thing the writer wants me to know?" Then, when you think you've figured it out, go back through the piece and see if you can find the key details that support your interpretation.

Miss Margot says

Sometimes, after you've finally picked out a main idea, you start writing and realize it's not actually the most important thing. That's okay. Just start over. Find the thing you've decided is most important and go with it. That's what better writers do all the time.

BUILDING A BETTER MAIN IDEA

Every piece you write should have a main idea. It doesn't have to be written down but your readers have to be able to figure out what it is. And that's why *you* need to know what it is whether you write it down or not.

The best way to come up with a main idea is to ask yourself, "What's the one most important thing I want my readers to know?" The answer should be:

- **A complete sentence.** If you're writing a piece about your vacation and you say the most important thing is "my vacation", that's not a main idea because it's not a complete sentence. What is it about *your* vacation that you want us to know? Maybe it's something like this: "Disneyworld in Orlando is the best vacation a family could have." That sounds like a strong main idea.

- **Something important to the writer.** Whatever you come up with, it has to be something you really care about. After all, if your message isn't important to you, it probably won't be important to your reader.

- **Something important to the reader.** This is the hard part. How can you know before you've finished a piece if your readers will think your message is important? You can't know for sure so you have to make a good guess. This means knowing who your readers are and why they might want to read what you've written.

A good piece of writing isn't just a loose list of ideas, it's a focused collection of information organized to support a central message. Readers depend on this structure to follow along and to sort out the things that are important from those that are not.

MEAT ON THE BONES

Speaking of vacations, I just took one. Why don't I write a piece about it?

My Vacation

I took a vacation. I got to see some interesting things. I ate some good food. I had a lot of fun. I hope I get to go back.

The End

Okay, what's the problem here? My piece looks a little thin, doesn't it? Seems like I need to put some meat on those bones.

This is what details are for. Details are the meat of any piece of writing, they're what readers like to sink their teeth into. Without details, a piece looks scrawny and unappetizing, like it's just a pile of bones.

And that's what my piece looks like: no meat, all bones. You might think this is an unusually bad piece of writing. And if you did, you'd be at least half right. It sure is bad, but it's not unusual. I get pieces like this from students all the time. They don't want to put any meat on either. Everybody wants to be skinny these days. And while that's good for your health, it's not good for your writing. So we have to figure out how to fatten things up.

Read Like a Reader:

How Fat Should Writing Be?

Kids always ask me, "How many details do we need?" And I always give them the same unsatisfying answer: "As many as your reader needs." There's no specific number of details that will always work. But you can get a sense of what good writers do by studying how they solve the problem. Take any piece of writing and ask yourself, "How many details does this writer give me when he or she introduces a new idea?" Sometimes it's hard to get an exact count but you can always get a sense of the number of sentences or the number of words the writer uses in certain situations to make sure that readers get enough detail without getting too much.

LOOKING FOR DETAILS

The first place to look for details is in the mind of your readers. One reason my piece is bad is because it doesn't tell my readers the things they want to know. Their minds are probably filled with questions. So that's the first place I'm going to go looking.

For each sentence I've written, I'm going to pretend I'm the reader and think about the questions I'd want the writer to answer:

- **I took a vacation.** Where did you go? How did you get there? Who went with you? How long did you stay? Why did you go there?

- **I got to see some interesting things.** What kinds of things? Why were they interesting? What was the most interesting thing?

- **I ate some good food.** What kind of food? Was it good? Was it expensive? What restaurants did you go to?

- **I had a lot fun.** Why was it fun? What was the most fun?

- **I hope I get to go back.** Why do you want to go back? How would it be different the second time?

Now my job is to try and answer these questions. Do I have to answer them all? No. But I need to consider all of them and answer the ones that I think are most important. This is going to generate a lot of information, so I'm going to use a strategy called Idea-Details to keep things organized.

ACTIVITY: WHO HAS QUESTIONS?

Since you're not the reader of your own pieces, coming up with the questions can be hard. Fortunately, you don't always have to do it by yourself. Just about anyone who understands what you're writing can fill in as a potential reader. Ask someone to read your piece and to tell you what questions they have as they go along. Don't take time to answer them; just write them down. You can add them to your piece after your reader is finished.

THE IDEA-DETAILS STRATEGY

I'll start by writing each sentence on the left side of an Idea-Details chart. Then, on the right side, I'll make a list of details by answering the questions I think my readers would ask.

IDEA	DETAILS
I took a vacation.	My wife and I spent three days in Asheville, North Carolina.
	It was about a four-hour drive.
	We went because my wife had always wanted to see the famous Biltmore Mansion at Christmas time.

IDEA	DETAILS
I got to see some interesting things.	The Biltmore Mansion and the Biltmore Estate.
	The winners of the National Gingerbread Baking Contest.
	The fanciest McDonald's I've ever seen.
	The scenery in the western part of North Carolina.
I ate some good food.	We stopped for lunch in Winston-Salem at a popular restaurant called "Sweet Potatoes."
	We had a tasty vegetarian lunch in downtown Asheville.
	We bought sweet snacks to take back to our hotel.
I had a lot of fun.	It was very relaxed.
	We slept in late and stayed up late, too.
	Visiting the Biltmore Mansion was very interesting.
	We went to Waynesville where I bought a life-sized stuffed Black Lab because it looked just like our dog, Ursa.
I hope I get to go back.	It might be interesting to see the mansion again at another time of year.
	If we save a lot of money, some day we might be able to stay at the inn on the Biltmore Estate.
	There were lots of little places to drive to that we didn't have time to see.
	I might be able to do some trout fishing in the mountains.

All of a sudden, it seems my scrawny little piece isn't looking so scrawny. Turns out I've got tons of details, probably even a few I don't need. But wait, there's more!

ANOTHER WAY TO USE THE IDEA-DETAILS STRATEGY

I love using the Idea-Details strategy because it's so fast and so easy. I can even use it on itself. Take this Idea-Details chart, for example:

IDEA	DETAILS
I got to see some interesting things.	The Biltmore Mansion and the Biltmore Estate. The winners of the National Gingerbread Baking Contest. The fanciest McDonald's I've ever seen. The scenery in the western part of North Carolina.

Because the Biltmore Mansion was the highlight of the trip and the main reason we went, it would probably be a good idea to include more details about it. To do that, I'll move it from the "Details" side over to the "Idea" side of a new chart:

IDEA	DETAILS
The Biltmore Mansion and the Biltmore Estate.	It was as big as a castle. It had 255 rooms. It was the largest family residence in the U.S. It took six years to build. It was decorated with beautiful Christmas trees in many of the rooms. It had very large round bedrooms.

I could go on and on. And that's just what the Idea-Details strategy is all about. It gives you the opportunity to create large lists of details and then decide how and if you want to use them.

PERFECT FOR PRE-WRITING AND REVISION

The Idea-Details strategy is perfect for fleshing out pieces early in the writing process. In just a few minutes, you can turn a few sentences into a few paragraphs. But Idea-Details is also great to use during revision. Here's a simple five-step process you can use in any piece you write:

5

1. Find a sentence that cries out for details.

2. Put that sentence on the "Idea" side of an Idea-Details chart.

3. Think of the questions your readers would ask.

4. Write the answers in the "Details" column.

5. Turn your details into complete sentences and insert them back into your piece.

Even though the Idea-Details strategy is a simple one, don't think it isn't valuable. It's fast, it's easy, and you can use it in almost every piece you write.

ACTIVITY: THE ONLY STRATEGY YOU NEED

Any piece of writing can be broken down into a set of Idea-Details charts. As an exercise, try writing an entire piece this way. Start with your first idea and put some details down. Then either pick a detail and make it your next idea, or come up with a new idea and add details to that. Idea-Details might be the only strategy you need.

Read Like a Writer:

Use Idea-Details for Note Taking

I just said that any piece of writing can be broken down into a set of Idea-Details charts. This means you can also use Idea-Details to organize and remember what you read. The Idea-Details strategy is perfect for what some people call "split-page note taking." This means that as you read, you put the important ideas on one side of the chart (or page) and the supporting details on the other.

But what if you come to an important spot in a piece, a place where you know you'll need lots of detail, and you don't have anything written yet? Where will your details come from then? Let's find out.

WHERE DO DETAILS COME FROM?

This happens to me all the time: I get to an important scene in a story, a scene I really want to write well, and I just blank out. I know the ideas I want to write about but I can't come up with the details.

To give you an example of what I'm talking about, consider this situation: I'm working on a piece about a big car accident I had a few years ago. I'm right at the part where the other guy hits me. This is the most important part of the story, so I want it to contain lots of good detail. But where will those details come from?

DETAILS COME FROM CATEGORIES

I like to think of details as coming from different categories like actions, feelings, setting, sights, sounds, thoughts, and so on. To generate details, I think of a category and write down what comes to mind.

Here's how it could work in the car accident story. I'm stopped on the freeway in a traffic jam and a big truck hits me from behind. That's the scene. Now, to get the details, I go through the categories:

- **Actions:** I grip the wheel tightly and brace myself for impact. He slams on his brakes, swerves to the right, and peels off the passenger side of my car. My car lurches forward but only a little. His truck stops right beside me in the next lane. We both look over at each other.

- **Feelings:** At first I was bored and frustrated waiting behind the car in front of me. But then I got a funny feeling something was going to happen. When I knew the truck was going to hit me, I honestly felt like I was going to die. But it wasn't like that. I wasn't terrified or panicky; I was strangely calm, almost resigned to my fate. After he hit me, I was relieved. And then, a minute later, I got mad because my car was wrecked. At the same time, I was glad no one was hurt.

- **Setting:** It was early morning rush hour. I was on Interstate 5 just south of Seattle. It was a typical dark gray day.

- **Sights:** After the crash, there was glass and metal all over the highway. The entire right side of my car had been stripped off. Other cars were whizzing past us at sixty miles per hour.

- **Sounds:** The engine roar of the truck that was going too fast to stop. The screech of brakes. The crash and scrape of the truck running into me. The clang and crunch of metal and glass raining down on the highway as passing cars kicked up the debris.

- **Thoughts:** What's that sound coming up behind me? I think I'm going to die. My mom would be so sad if I got hurt or was killed. Wow, I can't believe I'm okay. I wonder if the other guy's all right? Hey, my car is still drivable!

Using these categories, it's easy to come up with good details. And if I need more, I can either think up other categories (like objects or dialog, for example) or add more details to the categories I already have.

Working this information into the piece is easy. All I have to do is arrange the sentences into paragraphs.

> Sitting motionless on the freeway, stuck behind a line of cars in morning rush hour, I felt bored and frustrated. Then I heard something coming up behind me. A truck. Not slowing, not stopping, the roar of its engine growing by the moment. I gripped the wheel and braced myself for impact. I thought I was going to die.
>
> I had always imagined that in a moment like this I would be terrified and panicky. But I wasn't. I realized there was nothing I could do, so I did nothing. The only thought that came to mind was of my mother. I knew how sad she would be if I got hurt or was killed.

With this approach, it's easy to pick details from different categories and put them together into paragraphs that tell an interesting story. We want our readers to experience a wide range of details from as many different categories as we can think of.

Read Like a Writer:

What Categories Do Other Writers Use?

Find a spot in a book you're reading that has very detailed description. As you read each detail, ask yourself what category you might put it in. Many of the details you find will belong in the categories we've already discussed, but some won't. These are the ones you want to pay attention to because this is how you can learn about other ways of adding details.

Details are the heart of good writing. So it pays to have several ways of adding them to a piece. We now have three:

3

1. **Thinking about the reader's questions.** This should always be your first detail strategy because it takes you into the mind of your reader. Often, it will be the only strategy you need.

2. **Using the Idea-Details strategy.** This is the best strategy when you want to elaborate on something you've already written.

3. **Going through categories.** This the best strategy when you know you need detail but don't have anything written yet. It's probably also the best strategy for stretching your abilities because the categories can prompt you for details you don't normally think of.

But there's one more detail strategy that might just be the best strategy of all.

THE "SHOW ME" STATE

They call Missouri the "Show Me" state. Apparently, if you go up to a person from Missouri and tell them something, they won't believe you right away. "Show me!" they'll say, and you'll have to produce your proof right there, or they just won't take you seriously. Over the years, the phrase, "I'm from Missouri," has come to mean that a person is not easily convinced about things until they see the proof.

Readers are from Missouri, too. They won't just take your word for it; you gotta show 'em. But how can you do that when all you have are words? For example, in my car accident story, it's not as if I can bring each reader out onto the highway to see what happened.

This is where the Tell-Show strategy comes in. Instead of just telling my readers that my car got smashed in a bad accident, I'll show them by substituting rich description:

TELL	SHOW
My car got smashed in a bad accident.	The truck driver slammed on his brakes and swerved to the right.
	He hit my right rear fender and kept going forward right along the passenger side of my car.
	The outside of my car crumpled up like an accordion.
	Glass and metal flew everywhere and came clanging down around us.

Now I'll string all these "showing" details together into a paragraph:

> I heard a loud screech as the truck driver slammed on his brakes and swerved to the right. But he didn't swerve far enough to keep from hitting me. His truck plowed into my right rear fender and kept on going forward all the way up along the passenger side. My car hardly moved at all as the body crumpled up like an accordion. As the truck came to a stop in the lane next to me, glass and metal came clanging down around us.

Notice that I'm not just writing up the words exactly as they are on the "Show" side of the chart. I'm changing them a little to improve the writing and to make the sentences flow more smoothly.

ACTIVITY: CLOSE YOUR EYES AND VISUALIZE

This may sound dumb but it really works. The next time you're trying to put in some "showing" details, think about your "telling" sentence, close your eyes, and make a picture in your mind. As the picture comes into focus, try to name all the things you can "see." Then open your eyes and write everything down. This is called visualization, and it's the key to great description. Nothing works better for creating vivid details.

Read Like a Writer

What's the Tell?

Great writers, especially when they're writing great fiction, do a fabulous job of "showing." Often they do it so well they don't tell us the "tell." That means we have to figure it out for ourselves through inference. The next time you come across some good "showing" detail, see if you can figure out what the missing "tell" would be. Not only will this help you learn about writing, it will improve your reading comprehension, too.

"Showing" is not easy. It takes a little practice. When I was learning how to do it, I looked for simple "telling" sentences that would be easy for me to describe. You can do that, too. For any of the following sentences, make a Tell-Show chart, put the "telling" sentence on the left, and write your "showing" details on the right:

- The weather was awful.

- The party was a lot of fun.

- The woman was angry.

- The house was falling apart.

- The game was exciting.

- The dinner was awful.

After practicing with sentences like these, look for similar sentences in your own writing. These are great opportunities to substitute more interesting "showing" language for simple "telling" language.

LET ME SHOW YOU HOW IT WORKS

"Showing" is easier to understand when you can see it in a whole piece of writing. In this piece about a wedding, written by Micaela Arneson, you'll find many good examples. Rather than just telling us what it was like to be a five-year-old at her aunt and uncle's wedding, Micaela shows us with rich descriptions of herself and of the setting.

The Wedding

It was the perfect day for a wedding. The sky was a soft light blue and the occasional breeze swept gently over the lawn. People clustered around the metal folding chairs set up on the grass, talking and laughing. Most of the guests I had never seen before, but I picked out my family members and ran to greet them, hugging them one by one. I spotted my uncle dressed in a smart-looking black suit. My aunt-to-be was in a long beautiful white gown. I felt like a pot of hot water on a stove: any minute now I was going to boil over with excitement.

After a little while, everyone started to take their seats and quiet down. All eyes were on my aunt as she walked up the grass toward my uncle. My legs thumped wildly against my chair, my fingers were tapping, and I started to bounce up and down in my seat. The ceremony lasted about a half hour, too long for me to keep my eyes from wandering around the yard. An enormous magnolia stood behind my uncle, its beautiful white flowers opening to the sky. To the right of all the chairs was the Horace Williams House, its yellow paint contrasting nicely with the magnolia.

Then the ceremony was over as the final words were said, and everyone started to get up out of their seats and head for the house. Soon, the cake was brought out, a beautiful three-layer vanilla cake with white icing and perfectly-shaped flowers. It was a work of art; I was almost sad to eat it. As soon as I received my slice, I headed back toward the chairs to sit down and eat with my little brother. While shoveling cake into my mouth, I spilled a small sliver of it onto my pretty plaid dress, the dress I wanted to wear for my kindergarten graduation the following month.

When we were finished, my grandpa took the two of us to the magnolia, stooping under its low branches. I was delighted to find that underneath the branches, a clear wide space circled all the way around the tree's gigantic trunk. We walked around and around the tree, enjoying the shade. After a few minutes, we came out to talk and laugh a little more with the other people. I felt so happy and calm; I now had a new aunt!

My family seemed very happy as well, chatting amiably with my aunt and uncle, and congratulating them. When my aunt and uncle were ready to leave, I grabbed my basket of flower petals, and my little brother grabbed his bubble tube. Together, we threw and blew our petals and bubbles at my aunt and uncle as they got into their car and left the wedding. Eventually, my family got into our car and we drove home, excited, tired, and happy.

As an older and more mature person now, my outlook on that day is very different. It was a happy and blissful beginning, no doubt, but it led to a not-so-happy and not-so-blissful end. My uncle and aunt encountered several obstacles in their life together and, unfortunately, they could not overcome them. After marriage counseling and several attempts to work out their differences, my aunt and uncle divorced five years later.

Unfortunate as it was, their marriage and divorce has been a good learning opportunity for me. If I have any future relation-ships, I will be sure to be kind and considerate to my spouse, and always open-minded. I will treat my spouse with respect and give as much, if not more, as I take.

Right off the bat, Micaela starts with a wonderful Tell-Show lead: "It was the perfect day for a wedding. (Tell) The sky was a soft light blue and the occasional breeze swept gently over the lawn. People clustered around the metal folding chairs set up on the grass, talking and laughing." (Show) Then, just below in the same paragraph, she describes her state of mind: "I felt like a pot of hot water on a stove: any minute now I was going to boil over with excitement." She could have just told us she was excited. But instead she gives us a simile ("like a pot of hot water on a stove") to show us how she felt.

WHY ASK WHY?

Everyone talks about how hard it is to start a piece of writing, but knowing when you're finished is probably even harder. Often, in the real world of professional writing, we're told that a piece can't be longer than a certain number of words. Reach that number and you're done. Or maybe you're not. There's more to finishing a piece than just getting the length right.

A piece of writing has to accomplish something. Take this book, for example. It's made up of many different smaller pieces arranged as individual sections, most of them between 500 and 1500 words long. While I do keep an eye on the length of each section, I don't just hit a certain number of words and stop. Why? Because each section I write has a purpose, and I don't stop until I think I've achieved it.

In general, my purpose in each section is to teach you something about writing. But within each section, I have a more specific purpose related to a specific concept or technique I want you to learn. In the previous section, for example, I wanted you to learn to use the Tell-Show strategy. I also wanted you to understand the value of "showing" and how it is often better than just "telling."

WHAT IS PURPOSE?

This is how I've come to think about purpose in my writing: the purpose of a piece is what I want my readers to think and/or do. Knowing this keeps my writing focused and keeps me on track as I go along. It also makes it possible for me to know when I've reached the end, regardless of how many words I've written.

Purpose in writing can be hard to understand. While we can certainly read an author's words, we can't read an author's mind. In that sense, we can only guess about the author's purpose. Even when we're the author, we might not be able to put our finger on it. Or we might just be writing for no reason at all.

Another thing that makes purpose hard to understand is the way we talk about it in school. Our teachers often tell us that the purposes of writing are to explain, to persuade, to entertain, to describe, or to tell a story. This may be true in theory, but in practice it isn't very helpful. In any case, professional writers rarely talk about it this way.

School also presents another problem for us in understanding purpose. More often than not, when we're writing in school, we're not writing for a purpose, we're writing for a grade. Writing for grades in school is just a fact of life. But it can make discovering real purposes for our writing more difficult.

PURPOSE MAKES YOU BETTER

One way to be a better writer is to be more purposeful about your writing. For example, I often write newspaper editorials. I know that in order to get published, my piece has to be between 650 and 750 words, and that I have to be sure about what I want my readers to think and/or do. So I need to be focused, clear, and concise. Knowing my purpose, and working to accomplish it in a specific number of words, makes me work hard. I write and re-write, making many small changes. With each change, I try to make the piece a little better and a little more likely to achieve my purpose. The harder I work at being purposeful in my writing, the better I seem to get. In fact, I might even say that the *only* times I've gotten better at writing are times when I've been writing for a specific purpose.

GOT PURPOSE?

If you're starting to write something and you're not yet sure of your purpose, don't worry about it. For one thing, you may not know what your purpose is until you get farther along. But as you get close to finishing a first draft, ask yourself, "Why am I writing this? What do I want my readers to think when they're finished reading? What do I want them to do?"

Miss Margot says

Purpose in my work is the "Who cares?" question. After I come up with an idea, I have to be able to figure out a reason someone should care about the topic. Otherwise, it's just another story about the same old stuff. And nobody wants to read that.

Admittedly, it's easier to find a purpose in some kinds of writing than it is in others. For example, when I read the directions for a product I've purchased, it's very easy to understand the writer's purpose. But when I read a novel, it's harder to describe. Novelists are purposeful writers, too, of course. Fiction writers often have a purpose related to helping us learn something about life and the world around us.

As you sit down to work on your next piece, think about why you're writing it. What do you want your readers to think and/or do? Then write with that purpose in mind, and when you think you've gotten it down, stop. Don't write another word. There's no need to go beyond what you set out to do. If things don't seem quite right, make changes. But make them for the conscious reason of improving how well your piece achieves your purpose. This is how you'll get to be a better writer.

ACTIVITY: KNOW YOUR PURPOSE

Just as you do with your main idea, it's good to keep your purpose in mind as you write. In some cases, you may feel your purpose is the same as your main idea. Nothing wrong with that. But often it will be different—something that relates to or enhances your main idea but not the same thing. Your purpose can also inspire your ending. Just ask yourself what you want your readers to think and/or do after they've read your piece and say that at the end.

Read Like a Writer:

Determining an Author's Purpose

As you read, try to keep track of the author's purpose. This is not easy. You can't ask the author directly, nor can you read the author's mind. So you have to make an educated guess. Ask yourself these questions: Why did the writer write this? What does the writer want me to think? What does the writer want me to do? You may not come up with an answer that really works, but going through the process of thinking about purpose will increase your understanding and enjoyment of what you read.

A SURPRISE IN EVERY BOX

Do you know why they put toy surprises in boxes of cereal? They don't do it to improve the taste, that's for sure.

Everybody loves surprises. Let's face it, life can be boring. Every day is pretty much the same as the one that came before. And even though we grow and change over the course of our lifetimes, it's not as if we can see or feel it happening minute by minute.

So we enjoy little surprises now and again. Readers do, too.

Let's say you're writing about your birthday party. Your readers have had birthdays, too, or course. What can you bring to this piece that will surprise them? (And don't tell me you had a surprise party—that's not what I'm talking about.)

Coming up with interesting and unusual elements for a piece of writing is not easy. In fact, I would say most of us fail at it most of the time. That's why it seems most writing is pretty much the same as any other writing. But this doesn't mean we have to give up trying to present unique ideas in new and exciting ways.

To help you with this difficult part of writing, try to keep certain questions in mind. You don't have to run through these every time you write. But they should always be there in the back of your brain encouraging you to write in ways your readers will find refreshing:

- How is the way I think about this topic different from the way my readers think about it?

- How is the way I am presenting information in this piece different from the way my readers have seen it presented before?

- How is my life experience different from my readers' life experience?

- How is my personality different from my readers' personality?

- How can I make my writing different from what my readers expect?

You can tell, because it comes up in every question, that the key word here is "different." But that's just part of the deal. After all, we can't be so different that we put our readers off. This is where it gets tricky. If we go too far, our readers may think we're being silly or weird—or even worse, we may offend them.

The secret is to be different in a way that works for your audience. This requires two things: knowing your readers and taking risks with your writing. This is where good friends, great teachers, and patient fellow writers come in handy. When you're trying something that's a little different, you need to get feedback from other people before it goes out to the public.

Perhaps the best advice you could consider about creating writing that's surprising and original is simply to write from the deepest place in your personality and be willing to reveal who you really are. You are a unique individual after all. No one is exactly like you. And no one can write exactly like you—as long as you're not trying to write like someone else.

BE A WRITER LIKE LORI BAKER

Lori Baker is a public relations/publications writer for Baylor College of Medicine in Houston, Texas. Her interest in medical discoveries directed her career path toward several academic health organizations including Duke University Medical Center in Durham, North Carolina, and the University of Texas Medical Branch in Galveston. Although her career has primarily focused on producing printed materials, she also spent a few years in corporate communications as the human resources communications manager at Duke.

Q WHAT KIND OF WRITER ARE YOU?

A I'm a publications writer. I write text for brochures, magazines, and newsletters for a medical school. A big part of my job is telling other people about the medical discoveries and other cool stuff going on at the school. Sometimes I act like a reporter, so my writing is factual. Other times, I get to be more creative, like someone in advertising.

Q WHY DO YOU WRITE?

A I write because it's fun. I enjoy learning about things, figuring out what details are the most important and interesting, and finding the best way to get that information across to other people. I also enjoy that other people get something out of my work—they gain information.

Q

A

Q

A

WHAT MADE YOU WANT TO BE A WRITER?

I remember when I was doing writing assignments in school how satisfied I felt when I found just the right words to express my ideas. I still feel that way when I write, so I get a tremendous amount of satisfaction from my job.

WHAT ADVICE WOULD YOU GIVE TO A FELLOW WRITER WHO IS JUST STARTING OUT?

Volunteer your services to build your portfolio and contacts. Sadly, there are not many people who are good writers, yet every organization needs people to help them communicate. Writing for non-profit organizations or other groups you are interested in is a win-win situation—you gain experience to help you land jobs and they get their message out.

CHAPTER FOUR

Better Organization

TEN THINGS YOU NEED TO KNOW
EVEN IF YOU DON'T READ THIS CHAPTER

1. Organization in writing refers to five things: beginnings, endings, sequencing, pacing, and transitions.

2. A good beginning has to get your readers' attention and make them want to read more.

3. The beginning is the most important part of your piece because if it isn't good, readers may not read the rest.

4. A good ending has to feel finished and give your readers something important to think about.

5. Endings are much harder to write than beginnings, but it's important to write them well because the last words your readers read are the words they are most likely to remember.

6. In narrative writing, there are many ways to order the things that happen. You don't always have to start at the beginning and stop at the end.

7. Deciding on the order of things in non-narrative writing can be harder than in narrative writing because you don't have a timeline to follow.

8. Pacing is related to importance. Writers can slow down the pace by adding more details when they get to an important part. They can quicken the pace by using fewer details in less important parts.

9. The best transition is no transition at all. Whenever possible, put the parts of your piece in a logical order that your readers can follow without transitional phrases.

10. Using headings as transitional elements is the easiest way to move from section to section in a piece.

LET'S GET ORGANIZED

Anyone who knows me knows I'm incredibly disorganized. My desk is a mess. My office is in chaos. And I couldn't use a filing cabinet if my life depended on it. It's not that I'm opposed to organization, I just never think about it. I guess I'm too busy making a mess to worry about cleaning it up.

My writing used to be like that, too. I never thought about how I was going to organize my ideas in a piece. I just started writing at what seemed to be the beginning and tried to stop at what seemed to be the end—not exactly an approach I could rely on to produce good results.

My problem was that I never had any language I could use to talk about organization with other writers or to think about it on my own. It wasn't until I hit my thirties, and had been writing professionally for over ten years, that I took some classes about teaching writing and got the help I needed.

One of the most important things I learned was that organization isn't as complicated as I once thought. In fact, it boils down to five essential things:

- **A beginning that catches your readers' attention and makes them want to read more.** Different kinds of beginnings affect readers in different ways. We want to think carefully about the kind of beginning we choose, so we can draw our readers into the story and keep them reading beyond the first few sentences.

- **An ending that feels finished and gives your readers something to think about.** Endings are hard because they have to satisfy expectations readers have built up through the entire piece. It's not enough just to stop when we're out of material. We have to leave the reader with something that not only wraps things up but also explains why what we've written matters.

- **A sequence that puts each part of a piece in the best order.** The order we put things in has a huge impact on our readers. Even true stories about things that happen in our lives can be sequenced in different ways. We don't always have to start at the beginning and end at the end.

- **Pacing that allows for the right amount of time for each part of a piece.** For some parts of a piece, we need to write many sentences; for others, just a few. This affects the pace of our writing. Pacing is partly related to detail. In general, the more details we use, the slower the pace; the fewer details we use, the quicker the pace. (Pacing can also be affected by the kinds of sentences a writer uses. But I'll be talking more about this in Chapter 7: Better Sentences.)

- **Transitions that make a piece easy to follow from part to part.** Pieces are made up of parts. Transitions help readers find their way from part to part without getting confused. Sometimes we actually write strings of words called "transitional phrases" to let the reader know a new part is beginning. But if you put each part in the right order, and use thoughtful details, the reader can move through your piece simply by following the logic of your ideas.

Beginnings, endings, sequencing, pacing, transitions. That's organization. Of course, when you're stuck somewhere in the middle of a draft, it's not that simple. Knowing what these things are doesn't make you a better writer; it's knowing what to do with them that counts. But don't worry—that's exactly what we'll be covering in the rest of this chapter.

YOUR CHECKLIST FOR BETTER ORGANIZATION

You can be a better writer by having better organization. Take a piece you've written and see if it has the following elements. If it doesn't, use this checklist as a guide for revising it.

A piece of writing with good organization has five essential elements:

A beginning that catches your readers' attention and makes them want to read more. How does your beginning catch your readers' attention? Why would your readers want to read more? How will your readers know they are about to have a worthwhile experience?

An ending that feels finished and gives your readers something to think about. How does your ending make the piece feel finished? What will it make your readers think about? How does it let your readers know that what they've read is important?

A sequence that puts each part of a piece in the best order. Can your readers easily identify the different parts of your piece? Does each part follow logically from one to the next? How does the sequence keep your readers reading?

Pacing that allows for the right amount of time for each part of a piece. Why do you spend more time in some parts than in others? Are there places where you move ahead too quickly or hang on too long? Do the more important parts of your piece have more details than the less important parts?

Transitions that make a piece easy to follow from part to part. How do you move from part to part? How do these transitions help your readers follow the piece? Have you done everything you can to arrange parts in a logical order so transitional phrases are rarely needed?

Of these five elements, a strong beginning and a satisfying ending are probably the most important. Sequencing matters, too, of course, but often the sequence of a piece is suggested by the story you're telling or the ideas you're working with, so it may not require much thought. Pacing can be very subtle; it may not matter at all if the pieces you are writing are very short. Transitional phrases will often come to you naturally as you write or, if you put things in the right order to begin with, you may not need them at all.

Miss Margot says

When I'm writing articles for a newspa-per, magazine, or website, I often go through this kind of process to assess my organization. And if I don't, my editors make me! It may seem like more work than you're used to doing, but I promise that just these five tips alone will make your writing more interesting and easier to read.

AUSPICIOUS BEGINNINGS

Auspicious. Now that's an unusual word. Sounds like *suspicious*. So you're probably suspicious about why I used it. Well, it just happened to be the perfect word to say what I wanted to say.

According to my favorite online dictionary, *auspicious* means "marked by lucky signs or good omens, and therefore by the promise of success or happiness." So what do lucky signs and good omens have to do with writing the beginning of a piece?

The beginning of a piece is special because readers use it to decide if they want to read the rest. In the first few sentences, they're looking for a sign, some indication, however faint, that reading the remainder will be an enjoyable experience. The beginning is like a promise that says, "If you like this, you'll love the rest."

SCHOOL DAZE

When I was a kid in school, I didn't think about the beginnings of my pieces, so most of them started with boring lines like, "One day…," or "Last week…," or even worse, "Hi, my name is Steve and this is my story." I guess my teachers were happy I put down anything at all.

Even as I grew up, went to college, and started writing professionally, I didn't pay much attention to beginnings. I just started with the first thing that popped into my head. I never realized that good writers put so much effort into crafting their opening lines.

But you don't have to stumble along blindly like I did. There's so much to learn from the ways successful writers start their pieces. Often, the most artful writing in an entire piece will occur at the beginning. Serious writers spend serious time trying out many possibilities before settling on the exact words that seem just right.

Nowadays, as a reader, I pay close attention to how other writers' pieces begin. Sometimes, especially when I'm reading a newspaper or magazine, I'll read the beginnings of several different pieces in order to find the one I like best. I also try to remember the kinds of beginnings that seem most effective to me so I can use the same techniques in my own writing.

Read Like a Writer:

Looking at Beginnings

Start noticing beginnings. If you're reading newspaper and magazine articles, pay close attention to the opening paragraphs. If you're reading a novel, remember that each chapter has its own beginning. In the course of your everyday reading, you might come in contact with a variety of different beginnings. Each one is an opportunity to learn something new.

Students sometimes ask me how long the beginning of a piece is supposed to be. That's a fair question. Unfortunately, it doesn't have a fair answer. How long should the beginning be? That depends.

Different writers strive for different effects with their beginnings, and some of those effects take longer to develop in the mind of the reader. Sometimes, a single sentence is all a writer needs for a perfect launch.

More often, however, beginnings take several sentences or an entire paragraph to develop fully—some might even stretch to two or three.

Regardless of how long a beginning actually is, it has to do its work quickly. You may have only ten to fifteen seconds to win a reader over. That's maybe fifty to seventy-five words for the average adult, even less if you're writing for kids.

Because beginnings are so important, and because you have to create one for every piece you write, opening lines are an excellent thing to focus on in your quest to be a better writer. In fact, I might go so far as to say that you could improve your writing more by creating better beginnings than by focusing on any other single thing.

ACTIVITY: COLLECT YOUR FAVORITE BEGINNINGS

The best way to learn about beginnings is to study the ones other writers use. Start collecting beginnings you like. Whenever you see one, jot it down somewhere. After you've collected a dozen or so, look the whole group over and start modeling your beginnings after the ones you like best.

ACTIVITY: WRITE MULTIPLE BEGINNINGS FOR EVERY PIECE

Start writing more than one beginning for every piece. When I'm working in classrooms, I make kids write at least three. Some professional writers try ten to twenty before they settle on the one they like best. Not only does this give you different choices for starting a piece, it generates interesting material you can often use later on.

Miss Margot says

In journalism, we make a distinction between the "lead" and the "top" of a story. The lead is usually just the first sentence or first paragraph, while the top is really the entire beginning as a whole. When I write an article, I don't just think about that first sentence or first paragraph, I think about the entire top of the story. Focusing on the whole way I want to get the story rolling guarantees it will be interesting enough for people to keep reading once they get past my lead.

TEN AUSPICIOUS BEGINNINGS

Learning from the beginnings other writers use is one of the best ways to get better. You'd be amazed at how many you come across in an average day. Most aren't anything special. But some will be perfect examples of techniques you can borrow for your own work.

Below you'll find ten different kinds of beginnings. Each kind has a name that's easy to remember. I've also told you a bit about why I like them and why I think they work.

1. START WITH A QUESTION

> Do you hate homework? Do you wonder why it was even invented? Can you imagine how great it would be to come home in the afternoon and be able to watch TV, play video games, or have a snack without having to think about school?

If you ask your readers a question at the beginning, they will find themselves wanting to answer it, and this will draw them in. Sometimes, as in this case, you don't actually answer the question. In other situations, you might choose to answer immediately in the opening or gradually throughout the piece. The question beginning is one of the easiest to write. But don't use it too often or it will lose its effectiveness.

2. START WITH A SOUND

> Crack! The ball flew off my bat and sailed over the pitcher's head. Crash! The glass shattered as my home run hit the home across the street and destroyed our neighbor's living room window.

Starting with a sound is a simple but effective way to get your readers' attention. In this opening paragraph, the writer uses two sounds and a technique called "parallelism" to make the beginning even more interesting. Parallelism in this example refers to the fact that the two pairs of sentences have the same structure—a very short "sound" sentence followed by a longer "description" sentence.

3. START WITH A DESCRIPTION

> The campfire crackled. Glowing orange sparks shot into the sky and floated up until they cooled and faded away. Six friends huddled around the flames listening to the night.

Starting with a description is often a great way to set a mood. The people on this camping trip seem to be enjoying the outdoors. The writer is trying to pull us into the scene so we can hear the fire and see the sparks. The phrase "listening to the night" suggests that even though this group is feeling relaxed, they are also alert and paying attention to everything around them.

4. START WITH A THOUGHT

> This is it. I'm going to die, I thought to myself, as I closed my eyes, gripped the steering wheel tightly, and prepared for impact.

This is the opening sentence from my car accident story. Starting with a thought gets the readers' attention because normally we can't tell what other people are thinking. But with this technique, we can get inside someone's head and eavesdrop on a personal monolog. It's like listening in on a conversation we're not supposed to hear.

5. START WITH CONVERSATION

"We're moving."

That's what she told me. I couldn't believe it! I had just made the basketball team and was making more friends.

"What?!" I exclaimed.

Most of us can't resist listening in on a good conversation. That's why most readers like dialog. It's even better if you can introduce a conflict like the writer does here. I love how sparse the dialog is; it's only three words. But the writer gives us a great sense of how final the decision is and how frustrated the kid feels.

6. START WITH STRONG FEELINGS

My heart jumped up in my throat as I raised my fist. I was sweating like a pig and my knees felt weak. I was so scared about what might happen next that no one heard my timid tapping at the door. So I stood there, in the cold, waiting—anxious, confused, and embarrassed.

This writer is obviously dealing with many feelings, all of them bad. As readers we can't help but wonder why. And that's the key to starting with feelings. Even though we have no idea what has happened or what will happen next, we can still relate to the person in this scene because we've experienced the same feeling, or something like it, at some time in our own lives.

7. START WITH A LIST

Darkness. Kids running wild. Crazy costumes. All that candy. And scaring people. Of all the holidays in the year, I love Halloween the most.

Starting with a list is a great technique. It's one of the simplest ways to begin, and it always gets your readers' attention because you don't use complete sentences. Here, the writer gives us a list of descriptive elements without any context. We're left guessing about the topic. Each item in the list is a sentence fragment—a group of words that isn't a fully formed thought—and this adds to our feeling of wanting more information. Finally, the writer reveals the subject and, thankfully, gives us a complete sentence so we can feel that the trail of ideas has come to a proper stopping point.

8. START WITH THE PAST IN THE PRESENT

> It is Saturday, December 7, 1941. Some Americans are sleeping in. Others are up early for holiday shopping. At colleges around the country, millions turn their attention to football. Almost no one is thinking about war.

In the opening of this research paper on the Pearl Harbor attack, the writer is writing about the past but using the present tense. This pulls readers into the piece by giving us the feeling that the action is happening right now instead of long ago. This technique can make history come alive for your readers. But use it sparingly; it gets old fast.

9. START WITH AN INTERESTING STORY

> On a dark December night in 1776, as he led a barefoot brigade of ragged revolutionaries across the icy Delaware River, George Washington said, "Shift your fat behind, Harry. But slowly or you'll swamp the darn boat."

In addition to exhibiting some nice sentence structure, this beginning ends with something we don't expect to hear from the Father of Our Country. It's funny and it also serves as a good example of the writer's thesis for this research paper: that George Washington was a pretty normal guy and not the aloof, untouchable leader we often imagine. The writer is using a technique called an "anecdote." An anecdote is a little story within a larger piece that serves as an example of an important point.

10. START WITH FANTASY OR FAIRY-TALE LANGUAGE

> In the good old days, long, long ago, when most movies were black and white, and popcorn only cost a nickel, my grandpa used to take me every Saturday to a double-feature show.

This is the opening to an essay where a kid reminisces about his grandpa. The beginning stands out because he writes it up as though it happened long, long ago in fairy-tale time. It's a true story, but this type of beginning fictionalizes it just a bit, and that makes it sound like it's going to be more fun than the typical "When I was a kid" essay. This style of beginning gives the piece a child-like, mystical quality that fits the subject matter perfectly.

Miss Margot says

I use many different types of beginnings in my articles, but my favorites are the question lead and the story lead. I use these especially when I'm stuck or short on time because I know they will work for almost any article. Sometimes I'll use them to help me get into a story I'm not excited about. Once they've helped me get started, I can go back later and write a different lead that's more effective.

HAPPY ENDINGS

Has this ever happened to you? You go to a movie, one you think you're really going to like. It starts out great and gets better and better. You think it's one of the best movies you've ever seen. Until the last minute. The ending is so disappointing that you walk out of the theater feeling bad, like you got ripped off.

We've all had this experience at one time or another. And it just goes to show how important—and powerful—endings can be. You can like ninety-nine percent of a movie, but if the one percent you don't like is the last one percent, the whole thing seems ruined.

It's the same with writing.

Just like moviegoers, readers want the experience of feeling satisfied at the end. That's not always easy. As writers, we often work on a piece for a long time and then, at some point, we just feel like stopping. It's as if we want to go back to the good old days when we were in kindergarten and every story ended with "The End."

But that won't get the job done now.

So what's a hard-working writer to do? You have to have an ending for every piece you write. And it has to be a good one. That's a lot of pressure to deal with. And pressure doesn't always make your writing better. So let's think a little about reading, instead.

Everything you read has an ending. Novels have endings for every single chapter. By paying attention to the endings you experience as a reader, you'll get a better sense of how to produce them as a writer.

Read Like a Writer:

Looking at Endings

Start noticing the endings of the things you read. Flip through a magazine and read only the last few paragraphs of each article. Or hit the web and scroll to the bottom of each page. It's better, of course, to read an entire piece and then read the ending. But you'd be surprised how much you can learn through studying endings all by themselves.

One thing you'll start to notice about endings is that they all have a certain feeling to them. A good ending just *feels* right. This is not an easy thing to pick up as a reader, nor is it easy to master as a writer. But as you read more endings, and write more endings, you'll begin to know what that feeling is.

Endings are hard, no doubt about it. And sometimes the way we study them in school makes them even harder. When I was a student, my teachers told me that an ending was supposed to restate and summarize what I'd already written in a piece. That always seemed awkward to me but I tried to do it anyway, even though I didn't think it made sense to repeat something my reader had already read.

Later on, in college and then in the professional world, I discovered that restating and summarizing wasn't going to get me very far. Endings, I learned, needed to do more than merely repeat what the reader already knew. A good ending goes beyond what has already been written to give readers something interesting to think about. It should also show readers why what they've read is important. You can't do that by repeating yourself.

For all the challenges that endings present, we can count on having one thing on our side: the reader. Just like you want to see a great ending to your favorite movie, readers are rooting for you to end with something satisfying, too.

You don't always have to write a typically "happy" ending. But with every ending you write, you should try to make your readers happy. When your last words linger in their minds long after they've turned the final page, you'll know you've been successful and that your work has had an impact.

ACTIVITY: COLLECT YOUR FAVORITE ENDINGS

The best way to learn about endings is to study the ones that other writers use. Start collecting endings you like. Whenever you see one, jot it down somewhere. After you've collected a dozen or so, look the whole group over and start modeling your own endings after the ones you like best.

ACTIVITY: WRITE MULTIPLE ENDINGS FOR EVERY PIECE

Start writing more than one ending for every piece. When I'm working in classrooms, I make kids write at least two. Endings are harder to write than beginnings, so try to be patient with yourself. Sometimes you may find you can combine parts of two or three possible endings into a single perfect ending.

Miss Margot says:

There are times when I just can't get a story to end. I've said everything I have to say, but it doesn't feel like it's over. When I get stuck like this, I go back to my beginning and see if I can do a little trick called "bookending." Bookending means ending a story with the same thing you used to start it off. I don't mean reusing your opening word for word, or restating and summarizing your piece; it's more like giving the ideas in your opening a slightly different slant that reminds your readers of where they started out. For example, if you started with a question, can you answer it at the end? Or if you introduced a story, can you finish it off? Doing this helps you begin and end the story with a similar style or idea that literally holds your piece together just like bookends hold books together on a shelf.

TEN HAPPY ENDINGS

Just as we did with beginnings, let's look at ten great ending strategies, too. One thing you might notice is that they all have a similar feeling to them. Beyond just learning a few ending strategies, it's important to get to know what a good ending feels like because this is how most writers create them.

1. END WITH ADVICE

> There are many activities you can choose to make your birthday celebration an unforgettable one. But if you're thinking about skydiving, take my advice: Stop thinking. In years to come, I'm going back to good old cake and ice cream.

It just seems like part of being human to want to tell other humans how we think they should live their lives. As one of my favorite sayings goes, "Take my advice. I'm not using it." But more to the point, it makes for a good ending. Readers want value from what they read, and some of that value can come in the form of advice you offer about an issue in your piece, especially if it's offered simply, cleverly, or with a special twist.

2. END WITH STRONG FEELINGS

> As I drove away, I was overwhelmed by my emotions. I was still shaking a little from the collision and I was angry that my car had been so badly damaged. But I realized I was also very thankful. A few feet one way or the other and I could have been killed. But I wasn't hurt at all. As strange as it seemed, I felt like this was the luckiest day of my life.

Sometimes, at the end of an important experience, we're left with very strong feelings. Describing those feelings, and trying to explain how they arose, makes for a satisfying ending, especially if the feelings we're describing are complex, contradictory, or in some other way surprising.

3. END WITH SOMETHING YOU WANT YOUR READERS TO DO

> Make a commitment to getting in shape today. Turn off the television, put down whatever it is you're reading (unless it's this essay, of course), and start living a healthy life right now. You'll be glad you did.

This type of ending can be very powerful. Telling your readers to go out and do something is a big deal because most of us don't like to do the things other people tell us to do. But if what you have to say is important, this type of ending might be just what you're looking for.

4. END BY TALKING ABOUT THE FUTURE

> Last year was definitely the hardest, craziest year of my life. And I loved it! Things are going great. I never knew the incredible feeling of accomplishing things that in the past seemed impossible—not only with school, but with my entire life. Every day is another chance to do something great. And now I have the confidence and motivation to conquer anything in front of me. I feel I owe this to many things and to many people, but most of all I owe it to myself. Now I think about the consequences of everything I do and say. And this helps me make better decisions, decisions that help me build a better future. The future! For the first time I'm looking forward to it.

In this essay, the writer has just come through a long set of challenging experiences and is looking ahead to a better life. Most of us think about our hopes for the future all the time. It's a normal, natural thing. And I think that's why this type of ending feels normal and natural, too.

5. END WITH SOMETHING YOU LEARNED

> I learned that I shouldn't lie because it gets me into worse trouble. If I'm ever in this situation again, I'm not going to lie. The next time I have a problem, I'm going to tell someone about it and ask for help.

This is the classic "moral of the story" ending most of us remember from when our parents read us bedtime stories. But if it's heartfelt, it makes a perfectly good ending for older kids and even adults, too.

6. END WITH A RECOMMENDATION

> Even after all the bad things that happened, it was still a fun evening and the food was delicious. If you go there, I can't guarantee you won't have all the problems we did. But I can recommend this restaurant to any family looking for something a bit out of the ordinary.

Much like the "advice" ending, the "recommendation" ending also tells the reader to go out and do (or not do) something. But it's a little friendlier. It feels more like a suggestion or an invitation than a demand.

7. END WITH A QUESTION

> Back in April, when they threw out the first ball, no one in Seattle expected such success. But as this miracle Mariner season comes to a close, the one thought on every fan's mind is this: Can they do it again next year?

If you can start a piece with a question, can you end a piece with a question, too? Why do writers use questions so often? Why are questions so effective in writing? Would it be possible to create a piece entirely out of questions? Does this paragraph give you any hints about that?

8. END BY HINTING AT A SEQUEL

> And so ends another after-school adventure—or misadventure, I should say. Stay tuned for more exciting escapades as a kid with not enough homework to keep him out of trouble, and way too many crazy ideas, battles boredom in the afternoon.

If you liked the original, you'll probably like the sequel, too. At least that's the thinking behind this type of ending. Writers love to be read.

And some are not merely content with the fact that you're reading their current piece—they want you to read their next piece, too. So they put a little advertisement for it right in the ending.

9. END WITH AN EVALUATION

> Sometimes disasters can be fun, and bad luck can bring people closer together. Even with all the trouble we had getting there, and the many unpleasant surprises we encountered during our stay, we all agreed that this was our best family vacation ever.

Often, when we find ourselves at the end of something, we want to make a judgment about it. We look back over the entire experience and ask ourselves: Was it good? Was it bad? How did things turn out? What's the bottom line? And if we find a good way to sum it up, our readers feel satisfied, too.

10. END WITH A WISH, A HOPE, OR A DREAM

> I hope someday I can be a good parent just like my mom. I don't know how she does it, how she always seem to know what to do when things go wrong, and how she stays so positive all the time. I guess there are a lot of things about parenting I have to learn. So for now, I'll just work on being a kid.

This is similar to the "future" ending but it's a bit more subtle and perhaps a bit more effective, too. Most of us have our own wishes, hopes, and dreams, so we can't help but identify with someone else's.

ORDER IN THE COURT

You've seen it a million times on TV. A lawyer questions a witness and things get tense. Then another lawyer jumps in with an objection. Observers in the gallery start yelling and screaming. Then we hear the piercing thwack of the judge's gavel and a voice booms out over everyone: "Order! Order in the court!"

If you don't put things in the right order, readers may judge your writing and find you guilty of confusion. The best organization requires that you choose the best sequence for the different parts of your piece. Sequencing refers to the order in which things occur—what comes first, what comes next, what comes after that, and so on. It isn't something we think about much. If we're telling a story, we just tell it from beginning to end. If we're presenting information, we often let the material organize itself. But in both cases, when we don't explore other options, we miss opportunities to make our case as strong as it can be.

SEQUENCING IN NARRATIVE WRITING

You can think of narrative writing as any kind of story writing, whether it's a true story, a story you've made up, or something in between. In narrative writing, we set out to tell a story from beginning to end in the order that it happens—or at least that's what the reader assumes. Playing with this assumption gives you a number of interesting organizational strategies to explore:

- **Move the beginning.** You don't have to start with the first thing that happens. In fact, you can start your story anywhere along the timeline representing its sequence of events. For example, if I'm writing about having a car accident on the freeway during morning rush hour, should I start when I wake up in the morning? When I first get into my car? When I hit the freeway? When I get stuck in a traffic jam? Each choice makes my story feel a bit different. The closer I start to when the accident actually happened, the more my story is likely to feel fast-paced and intense.

- **Move the ending.** Just like I can choose where to start, I can choose where to end, too. Should I end my car accident story when the truck hits me? When I drive my car away? When my car finally gets fixed? Or how about months later when I almost end up in an identical accident? Each choice gives the story a different quality.

The farther I move the ending from the accident itself, the less important the crash is likely to seem.

- **Start with the big moment.** Normally, stories start out slow and build gradually until they reach the most important part of the piece. I call this part "the big moment." In my car accident story, this is the moment when I was hit by the truck. What if, instead of putting that moment late in the story and building up to it, I started with it right off the bat? I'm sure this would get my readers' attention, and I might end up with an even more powerful piece.

- **Start with the ending and then go back to the beginning.** As strange as this seems, we come across it all the time. In my case, I would start with the fact that I had an accident and then go back and tell how it happened. Some mystery stories work this way when they are told by the main character. If you've read *The True Confessions of Charlotte Doyle* by Avi you know exactly what I mean.

- **Tell the entire story backwards.** This is hard but it can be done. I've seen it mostly on television and in the movies, where the visual medium can switch scenes easily.

- **Tell the story out of order (with clues).** Just because your readers assume a story is told in order, doesn't mean you have to tell it that way. You can jumble up the parts as much as you like, as long as you've left your readers enough clues to put the story back together in a satisfying way.

- **Tell more than one related story at a time.** Imagine if I told my car accident story from two different perspectives at the same time: mine and that of the guy who hit me. I could describe two seemingly unrelated stories and then smash them together just as the accident happens. Again, many books take a similar approach. *Holes* by Louis Sachar is a good example.

There's a lot more to narrative sequencing than just telling a story from beginning to end. But you have to explore your options. First, write down the simple chronology of events, and then play around with different beginnings, different endings, or even a different order altogether.

Read Like a Writer:

Newspaper Order

Newspaper stories, especially those you find on the front page or in the "A" section, are often written in an interesting order. Can you figure out how they work? Read several "straight news" stories from the first section of your local paper and see if you can figure out how the writers of these pieces planned their sequencing. How do you think they decided what should come first? How did they know where to end?

Miss Margot says

Figuring out what goes where can be hard. When I'm feeling challenged in this way, I just start somewhere, anywhere. I'll write one section and then another and then another. Sometimes, the order finds me. Other times, I get all the sections written, and then I have to move them around until the order feels right. Usually, I read all these versions out loud to see which one sounds the best. This is almost always the one that reads the best, too.

SEQUENCING IN NON-NARRATIVE WRITING

You can think of non-narrative writing as any writing that isn't a story. In this case, we're presenting different pieces of information about a topic as opposed to following something that happens along a timeline.

For example, instead of telling the story of my own car accident, imagine I'm writing a magazine article on the dangers of driving on the freeway during rush hour. There's no story here to tell, no single thing that happens. But I still have to figure out the best way to put my information in order.

Making decisions about what goes where in a non-narrative piece can be tricky. And often there's no right answer. But there are a few things we can think about to help us get the job done well:

- **Know all the parts of your story.** One of the things that makes narrative writing easier than non-narrative writing is that you don't need to have the entire story worked out before you start. If you want, you can just pick a starting point and tell what happened from there. But in a non-narrative piece, there is no "what happened from there." So before you can do much about your sequencing, it's helpful to know what each part of the story will contain.

- **Pick an interesting part to start.** Readers are very forgiving about the beginnings of narrative pieces. They know that stories often start out slow and build. But readers feel differently about non-narrative pieces. They expect to get interesting information right off the bat from their non-narrative reading, so we have to make sure we choose an interesting part to start with. One trick we can use is to start a non-narrative piece with a narrative. This is called starting with an *anecdote*. An anecdote is a very brief story (often just a few paragraphs) used to emphasize an important point. For example, my car accident story could be used in my magazine article as an example of how dangerous rush hour driving is.

- **Move from part to part through logical relationships.** In a narrative piece, we move from part to part simply by moving forward in time. But in a non-narrative piece, we don't have a timeline, so we have to use logic instead. This means trying to understand what readers are thinking as they read and giving them a logical reason, like a stepping stone, each time they move to a new part.

For example, if my magazine article contained a part with statistics about the most dangerous freeways in the area, and one of them happened to be the road where I had my accident, it might make sense to put those two parts next to each other.

- **Know what you're going to end with.** In a narrative piece, deciding on the ending is simply a matter of figuring out where to stop along the timeline. But in a non-narrative piece, just about any part of my story could be used as the end. To make my ending as effective as possible, I want to pick a part that will make a significant impact on my reader.

If you're thinking that sequencing narrative pieces is easier than sequencing non-narrative pieces, you're absolutely right. Telling a story simply involves following a timeline from beginning to end. Following logic is more complicated because you have to map out your thinking very carefully—and hope that your readers will be thinking that way, too.

Miss Margot says

I have to think about sequencing all the time. Most of the articles I write are about complicated issues like building houses for poor people, how much it costs to rent office space in a major city, or how businesses can better train their employees. There's no clear beginning or ending with that kind of stuff. What helps me wrap up the article is usually a quote, an idea from someone I talked to, or some research I did earlier that made me go, "Aha! I get it now."

In addition to using these strategies, there is one simple thing that usually works when I'm presenting non-narrative information to my readers: Explain things in the order that I figured them out. After all, before I could present the information, I first had to learn it myself. And though I probably didn't learn it in the ideal order, I eventually figured it out in a way that made sense to me. If I can describe it that way to my readers, it'll probably make sense to them, too.

Read Like a Writer:

Discovering the Parts

You can learn a lot about organization from digging into the organizational structures of the writing you read. But to understand organizational structure, you have to discover the parts the author used to compose a piece. To practice this, take a magazine article that runs three or more pages. With a marker, put a note in the margin each time the writer moves to a new part in the piece. As each new part begins, write down a word or phrase that tells what that part is about. If it's not obvious, complete this sentence, "This is the part about...." Notice how writers move from one part to another. Notice, too, how many parts there are in the piece and how long the parts are relative to the whole.

BE A WRITER LIKE LUIS J. RODRIGUEZ

Luis J. Rodriguez is one of the leading Chicano writers in the country with ten nationally published books of memoir, fiction, nonfiction, children's literature, and poetry. His poetry won a Poetry Center Book Award, a PEN Josephine Miles Literary Award, and Foreword *magazine's Silver Book Award, among others. His two children's books won a Patterson Young Adult Book Award, two "Skipping Stones" Honor Awards, and a Parent's Choice Book Award, among others. Luis is best known for his 1993 memoir of gang life,* Always Running: La Vida Loca, Gang Days in L.A., *an international best seller.*

WHAT KIND OF WRITER ARE YOU?

I write in various genres—poetry, children's books, novels, stories, journalism, essays, memoir, and now screenplays. I try to bring craft and rigorous work to my writing but also an emotional center. It's an odd combination of discipline and follow-through with levels of madness. At the root of my work is a revolutionary soul. I want to transform myself, my community, my world.

WHY DO YOU WRITE?

Why do I write? To heal. To dance. To wake up something beastly as well as something beautiful. I write to stay alive. I feel the most whole when I'm in a deep state of transcendental writing. Writing then is my practice, my career, my life line. I learned this when I was in jail. Turning to my art, I found what could save me. My writing always carries the wounds of my life; it's the gift these wounds have to offer.

Q

WHAT MADE YOU WANT TO BE A WRITER?

A

I first wrote while in jail and juvenile hall as a teenager. Something about telling my story overcame me. I felt the need to voice these experiences, these traumas, the depths of what I saw and where I had come to. At nineteen, I began to work in industry. I became a welder, pipe fitter, mechanic, carpenter, smelter, and a steel mill worker. Again, so many stories accumulated in me. The pressure of the stories was so great that, by age twenty-five, I decided to become a writer working in weekly and daily newspapers, in radio, as a freelance journalist, and as a poet. I went to school at night, took part in writing workshops and circles, and began this writing life that I've done now for more than twenty-five years.

Q

WHAT ADVICE WOULD YOU GIVE TO A FELLOW WRITER WHO WAS JUST STARTING OUT?

A

Writing is a practice, a passion, hard work, a business, a dream, and the most frustrating thing in the world. A writer must withstand all of this. Oh, yes, sometimes there's money and sometimes there's rec-ognition. But that's only sometimes. If you can't help writing, then write. Write all the time. And always read. Despite my sufferings and rages, I loved to read. In the streets. When I was homeless. In jail. I never stopped reading. And, of course, I still read in this calm family home environment I presently abide in. Reading has been the one constant. Beyond that you must never give up. Persistence is the true test. Do it no matter what. No matter what obstacles and sacrifices exist. It shows in the work. Those who breathe in and exhale words, who can't live without them, can't help but write life-affirming work. Write even when it seems the world says no. In every no, there's curled up a universe of yeses. The only art that matters is the art that is not supposed to be there.

PACE YOURSELF

When runners compete in long races like marathons, they have to pace themselves carefully. This means that at certain times in the race, they have to make sure they are going at just the right speed. Too fast at the beginning, and they'll tire themselves out. Too slow, and they'll be too far behind the leaders to catch up at the end.

Writers have to pace themselves, too. But instead of burning up energy, they burn up words as they move from section to section in a piece. You can think of the speed at which a piece of writing moves forward as being determined by the number of words a writer uses to describe a given part. The more words a writer spends on a part, the slower the piece moves along. When a writer moves from part to part with very few words, the pace quickens and the piece speeds up.

Here's a fast-paced approach to telling the beginning of my car accident story:

> I woke up and looked at the clock. I was late. I quickly threw on some clothes and ran out to the car. A few minutes later, I was on the freeway trying to make up for lost time. Then I noticed the traffic slowing down in front of me. Before I knew it, I was stopped. The people around me were turning off their engines. We were going to be here a while. But one engine behind me wasn't turning off. Instead, it was revving up. This was when I knew I was about to be hit.

And here's the same story told at a much slower pace:

> I woke up disoriented. Something was wrong; there was too much light. I looked at the clock and noticed I had slept well past the time I was supposed to wake up. I must have set my alarm wrong the night before, so I had to move quickly. I thought about taking a shower but figured I could save time if I skipped it. I found some clean clothes and put them on without worrying about how they looked. Then I hopped into the bathroom to brush my teeth and figure out what to do with my hair.

Both of these passages are ninety-eight words long. But the first one covers a much bigger chunk of the story than the second one does. In the first passage, I used my ninety-eight words to get myself up, out of bed, dressed, out to my car, onto the freeway, and stuck in a traffic jam right in front of a speeding truck that hasn't realized the cars in front of it are completely stopped. In the second passage, I didn't even get out of the house.

So how do you manage pacing in a story? In a word: *detail.* The more details you add to a part, the slower it goes by. This is good. When you're using many details, you can make your readers slow down and pay attention. But if you kept up the same heavy use of details in every part of a piece, your readers would get bored. This is when it's handy to thin things out and pick up the pace.

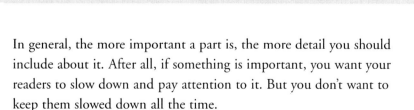

TIP:

As we'll see in "Chapter 7: Better Sentences," sentence length can also have an effect on pacing. In parts that feature many short sentences in a row, the pace will seem to quicken. Long sentences make the pace seem slower. But this is different than using details to control pacing. For one thing, writers can't write for very long using only short or long sentences. So it's hard to control the pacing for more than a paragraph or two with this approach.

In general, the more important a part is, the more detail you should include about it. After all, if something is important, you want your readers to slow down and pay attention to it. But you don't want to keep them slowed down all the time.

Readers, like runners, have to pace themselves, too, especially if they're reading something long. By controlling the amount of details you use, and by carefully mixing more detailed, slower-paced sections with lighter, faster-paced sections, you can make sure your audience reaches the finish line every time.

Read Like a Writer:

Embrace the Pace

The next time you sit down to read a story, make an effort to notice the pacing. First, try to identify the parts of the story as you move along. Then start asking questions. Where does the writer speed up and slow down? What's going on in the story when the writer uses more details? Why does the writer move quickly through some parts but not others?

PUTTING IT TOGETHER

You can think of a piece of writing as a collection of different parts. In my car accident story, for example, there's the part where I wake up late. Then there's the part where I get out of the house. Then there's the part where I'm stuck on the freeway. And so on. We can easily identify these parts as being separate from the rest but I don't have a whole piece until I put them all together.

So the question is, "How do you put different parts together to make a whole piece?" And the answer is, "With transitions."

Transitions help readers move easily from part to part without getting confused. To do this, readers have to know three things: when one part ends, when the next part begins, and what the relationship is between the two parts.

We often think of transitions as little words and phrases like "then" or "next" or "after a while." But that's only part of the story.

THE BEST TRANSITION IS NO TRANSITION

Ideally, we'd like our readers to be able to move from part to part simply because it makes sense to do so. If the first thing we write leads logically to the second, and the second to the third, and so on, our readers should be able to follow it without needing little words and phrases to string things together.

Take a look at this example from Chapter 1 of this book:

> I can still remember the first time I wanted to be a better writer. And sure enough, it had to do with Standard Adult Reason #2, getting into college. I was applying to transfer from the small school where I started to the big one where I *really* wanted to go. And I really wanted to go there. But I had to write two essays for my admissions application.
>
> The first college I attended had not required admissions essays. In fact, it required so little of me with regard to writing, I didn't have to take the required freshman and sophomore English classes. To make matters worse, I was a music major there. While I spent many hours writing music, I almost never wrote a sentence.
>
> There I was, twenty years old, needing to write a couple of sharp essays to convince a big university I was worthy of being admitted, and I discovered I didn't write very well. Truth was, I wrote okay. I was able to complete a slightly confused and rambling first draft of any essay I was assigned, but that was about it. In reading over what I'd written, I could tell my pieces had problems. But I couldn't figure out how to fix them. I didn't know how to make my own writing better, or how to make myself a better writer in the process.
>
> I spent weeks on my admissions application, fretting every moment about my essays, and was eventually accepted. Two years later I got my degree—in English no less, a subject where I had to write all the time. But struggling with those essays made it painfully clear to me that I needed to be a better writer. I wanted to be better, too, because I was beginning to see that writing well was the key to many interesting opportunities.

Each paragraph in this example is a different part of my piece. And yet I'm moving from part to part without transitions between paragraphs. How does that work? How am I connecting each new paragraph to the previous paragraph so my readers understand how the two paragraphs relate?

I'm using a strategy I call "referring back." Notice how each new paragraph refers back to something in the previous paragraph. This connects the set of paragraphs together like links in a chain.

Referring back is an easy strategy to use. (See, I just used it!) All you do is look back at the previous paragraph, pick out an important element you want to say more about, and refer to it in the new paragraph.

Each new paragraph (There I go again!) builds logically on the one that comes before. There's no need for transitional phrases, and your readers feel comfortable following along. If it was possible to write this way all the time, the whole topic of transitions wouldn't exist. But it isn't, so let's look at other approaches to moving from part to part in a piece.

Read Like a Reader:

Can You Find a Transition?

Great writers work hard to minimize the use of transitional words and phrases. Instead, they concentrate on writing so well that their pieces move smoothly and naturally from part to part without ever confusing the reader. Take a look at the novel you're reading now or some other high-quality writing. Look for transitional words and phrases. Can you find very many of them?

CONVERSATIONAL TRANSITIONS

If you were to tell someone a story about something that happened to you, you would naturally throw in transitions from time to time. Each time you got to a new part of your story, you'd introduce it with something like, "After we left the movie…" or "When I got home from school…" or "All of a sudden…." That's what transitions do—they introduce the next part of the piece.

While we should always try to move smoothly from part to part without using transitional phrases, there's nothing wrong at all with the occasional conversational transition. Conversational transitions sound normal and natural, just like you're speaking to the reader. And that's the key: if your transitions don't sound like you're speaking to the reader, you'll probably be able to hear it when you read it back, especially if you read it out loud.

SCHOOL TRANSITIONS

These aren't really called "school transitions" but I like to call them that because most people are introduced to them in school. At some point, if it hasn't happened already, your teacher will talk to you about transitions and give you a big list of transition words to study. These will be words like "then," "next," "finally," "but," "however," and "therefore." Your teacher may even tell you to use them to transition from paragraph to paragraph. This may or may not work for you. (It didn't work well for me.)

Of course, school transitions are legitimate transitions, and writers use them all the time. But I think the way we teach them to kids makes learning to use them very hard. If you're having a hard time with school transitions, remember that you've been using normal, natural conversational transitions all your life. Stick with those. That's what worked best for me.

TIP:

Regardless of what anyone at school tells you, you do not need a transition word or phrase to introduce each paragraph. In fact, doing this can make your writing seem repetitive and even immature.

HEADING TRANSITIONS

Perhaps the easiest transition to use is a good subhead, or what I like to call a "heading transition." Take a look at this entire section on transitions. See how I've broken it up into different parts by using different headings? ("The Best Transition Is No Transition," "Conversational Transitions," "School Transitions," and "Heading Transitions.") Instead of worrying about referring back or using a conversational transition or a school transition, I just end a part wherever I want to and plunk down a heading to begin the next part.

Heading transitions are very popular. You see them in newspapers, magazines, on the web, and in most kinds of nonfiction texts. They're also used a lot in textbooks. Headings are used less frequently in fiction and other types of narrative writing, but you'll still see them every once in a while.

Headings are helpful to readers because they clearly point out what's coming up next. They also make longer texts easier to scan because the reader can see the organizational structure and skip quickly from section to section to find specific information.

The only hard part about a heading transition is coming up with the right heading. A heading is really just a title. But it's a title for a single section, not an entire piece. If coming up with interesting titles is something you enjoy, I highly recommend using headings as your transition strategy of choice when moving from section to section.

Miss Margot says

Journalists are always looking for ways to get readers into the story, and that's why you see so many of us using "heading transitions." Fancy editors call them "points of entry," and not-so-fancy writers call them "subheads." Whatever you call them, they're not just good for transitioning, they're good for getting your reader's attention, just in case the headline or lead didn't. Subheads are usually offset in some way—with extra spacing, a larger font size, bold formatting, or all three—so they're hard for readers to miss. Having several points of entry in a story, especially if it's a long one, makes it easier for readers to find their way and stay engaged.

AN INTERESTING APPROACH TO ORGANIZATION

There really are many different ways to organize a piece of writing. For the most part, we just tell our stories in the order they occur to us. But sometimes writers take more unusual approaches. In the essay below, a writer tries something out of the ordinary. Do you think it works?

Two Girls

The girl huddles in a corner. It's late and she is cold. With only a tattered blanket to protect her, and no heat in the shack she calls home, she will spend the night sleepless and cold like she often does.

I sleep snug in my bed under a new comforter. Even though it's winter, I know I'll be warm all night long. And if I'm not, I'll just turn on my electric blanket or ask my parents to turn up the heat.

Longing for the sleep that never came, the girl steps outside. The sun warms her a little but not enough. Her clothes are rags. But the hunger in her belly is worse than the morning cold. She wonders, "How will I eat today?"

I wake up warm and toasty. The sun is streaming in through my bedroom window. It's a beautiful day. I put on my robe and slippers and head downstairs. I smell bacon and waffles cooking in the kitchen.

The hungry girl roams the streets begging for food, for money, for anything. People reject her. But she has been doing this for so many days she is no longer humiliated. Survival is more important than pride.

I feast on waffles and bacon. I drink orange juice my mom has just squeezed. I look forward to the day: soccer practice in the afternoon, a movie with friends at night. I wonder what I will wear.

Two girls, two lives. Why does one face every challenge while the other has every opportunity? Am I better than she is? What did I do to deserve the life I have? What did she do to deserve hers?

I think I can appreciate, now that I'm older, how lucky I am to have the life I have. When I was little, I thought everyone lived this way. But everyone doesn't. Unfortunately, I think I can also appreciate how unlucky other people are. I just don't know what to do about it.

Normally, when we contrast two things, we show one first and then the other. But the writer gets more out of the contrast here, I think, by weaving her two stories together in alternating paragraphs. This is not a technique a writer could keep up for many pages. But it works well in a short essay. Notice also that the writer creates an entire piece without using a single transition between paragraphs.

CHAPTER FIVE

Better Voice

TEN THINGS YOU NEED TO KNOW
EVEN IF YOU DON'T READ THIS CHAPTER

1. Voice is the element that makes every writer's writing unique.

2. Voice is choice. Each piece of writing is a set of choices—choice of topic, choice of ideas, choice of organization, choice of words, and so on. The choices that define a piece are like the fingerprint of the person who wrote it.

3. Voice is the most important quality in a writer's work because it influences almost everything a writer does. It's also the hardest quality to identify, manipulate, and improve.

4. The goal of improving your writer's voice is to make your writing more individual, more personal, more like you. A great way to do that is to put more emotion into what you write.

5. When readers can correctly identify you as the author of a piece of writing, you know your voice is coming through loud and clear.

6. The simplest way to think about voice is to think of it as personality.

7. If you're writing well, and your voice is strong, your work will reflect who you are. What your readers will notice is that your writing has some of the same personality traits you do.

8. In your social life, you know the behaviors and attitudes that are appropriate for different situations. The same idea applies when you write for different purposes and audiences.

9. Using the wrong voice with your readers can be a disaster. Imagine how you'd come across if you talked the same way in the principal's office as you talked with your friends at the mall.

10. Finding the right voice means balancing your need to express yourself honestly for who you are with your audience's need to be honored and respected for who they are and for the reason they are reading your work.

WHOSE WRITING IS THIS?

Voice, as a concept in writing, is not an original idea of mine; I did not invent it. It isn't even a new idea; people have been writing about it for years. In fact, I'll bet that much of what I'm going to say has already been said in many different ways by many different people at many different times. I may even use some of the same technical terms that other people have used to talk about it.

So whose writing is this?

Have you ever thought about the fact that when we write, we all have to choose what we want to say from the same batch of words? Our language certainly has many words to choose from, but most of us rely on the same small selection for just about everything.

So whose writing is this?

The topics we choose to write about may not differ that much either from the topics other writers choose. My vacation is similar in many ways to your vacation. Your story about your pet is probably a lot like my story about my pet. Even when we describe things about ourselves that we think are unusual, there are usually other people who could write similar things about themselves.

So whose writing is this?

There are literally hundreds of millions of people around the world writing in English every day. And many may be writing about exactly the same things. So how is it that one person's writing can seem so different from another's? What is it that makes a writer's writing unique?

Voice.

Sometimes referred to as style, mood, tone, or personality, voice is a part of writing that tells us something about who the writer is as a person. In fact, some people say, when they read writing that has a strong voice, it's as if they are getting to know the person behind the words.

For example, I just read Jerry Spinelli's *Maniac Magee*. I don't know Jerry Spinelli at all—never met him, heard him speak, or even read anything else he's written. But I feel like I know him now. I feel like he's a person who cares about the way people treat each other, a person who sticks up for the underdog, a person who wants everyone to get along and to play by the rules. But I also feel like he's a bit of a trickster. He's kind, funny, open-minded, and welcoming. But he knows the world can be a tough place and that you have to be able to protect yourself from tough people—or laugh things off when you can't.

That's a lot to know about a person—especially a person I've never met. And yet, after reading just one of his books, I feel as though I know him pretty well. I said I feel "as though" I know him. I don't really know Jerry Spinelli at all. What I know is Jerry Spinelli's voice in *Maniac Magee*. In this book, Jerry Spinelli writes "as though" he's a person with all the qualities I describe. It might be him, it might not, but as far as I'm concerned, it's definitely his voice as the writer of this book.

Read Like a Writer:

The "Who" of Writing

Think of an author whose writing you know well. Based on what you've read, what do you think about who this person is? What does this person believe? What does this person care about? What are this person's most significant personality traits? Is this someone you'd like to know? Why or why not? Try to tie the answers you come up with to specific parts of the writing you've read. And try not to base your opinions on things you may already know about the writer's life.

FINDING YOUR VOICE

So where's your voice? It's right inside you, of course. But finding it and getting it onto the printed page can be a challenge because we don't always know exactly where inside ourselves to look for it.

Are there certain words you use all the time? Are there certain phrases or expressions you like? Do you have a particular rhythm when you talk? These might be part of your voice as a writer. Do you have a special way you like to tell stories? Are there certain ideas, like themes in a book, that you keep coming back to over and over again? Things like these might be part of your voice, too.

Ultimately, voice is choice. You choose your topics. You choose your ideas. You choose your words. You choose where to start, when to stop, and what order to put things in. Each piece of writing is a set of choices. And the particular set of choices that defines a piece is like the fingerprint of the person who wrote it.

You're a unique person, different from all other writers. So it stands to reason that your writing will be unique, too. But only if you make choices that are true to who you are. If you write like someone you're not, you're going to end up with someone else's writing. After all, if every writer chose the same topics, the same words, and the same organizational structure, everything we read would be the same.

DESCRIBING VOICE

Voice can be a hard thing to describe. In fact, I don't think it has an official definition all writers would agree on. But many people would say that strong voice emerges when we sense the following five things:

- **The writer really cares about the topic.** One expression of your voice as a writer comes through when you write about things that matter to you. The topics you choose and the ideas you focus on are key elements of who you are as a writer.

- **The piece is filled with strong feelings and honest statements.**
To find your true voice as a writer, you have to be true to yourself
as a person. When you know exactly how you feel about things,
and you don't shy away from writing honestly about these feelings,
the words you choose are more likely to reflect your true voice.

- **The writing is individual and authentic.** Your writing should
sound like you—and nobody else. Your readers should feel like
you're right there talking to them. People who know you well
should be able to say that you sound the same on paper as you do
in person.

- **The writing displays a well-defined personality.** Your readers
should feel like they're getting to know you as they read your
work, just like I felt I was getting to know Jerry Spinelli when I
read *Maniac Magee.* Your personality should come through in your
writing, and your readers should be able to identify important
ingredients in it.

- **The piece has an appropriate tone for its purpose and audience.**
Voice isn't just about you expressing yourself. It's about you expressing yourself for a purpose to an audience. To reach your readers
successfully, sometimes you have to adjust your voice a bit. In this
case, your writing still reflects who you are, but how you present
yourself is influenced by why you are writing and who you are
writing to.

Voice is probably the most important quality in a writer's writing
because it influences almost everything a writer does. It's also the
hardest quality to identify, manipulate, and improve. People ask me all
the time what lessons and exercises I have for helping writers improve
their voice. And I always have the same answer: I don't have any lessons
or exercises.

The way to get better at voice is to get better at the things that make
your voice come through. Pick topics you really care about. Share
strong feelings. Write like you talk. Show off the best parts of your

personality. Respect the needs of your readers. Know who you are and bring that person with you every time you sit down to write. These are not things you get better at through a teacher's lessons or exercises in a workbook. But the more you write, and the more you think about these things, the more your voice will come through, and the better your writing will become.

Miss Margot says

When I write columns or opinion pieces, I get to sound like me. Even if you didn't read the byline, you'd know I wrote it because I use words and phrases in my writing that I use when I talk, and I make certain kinds of funny remarks (at least I hope they're funny). Anyone who knows me knows my words when they see them in print. And people who don't know me get a strong sense of who I am. But when I write feature stories or news stories, I'm not allowed to let my personality come through quite as much. These pieces have to sound pretty much like others in the same publication because the newspaper, magazine, or website I'm writing for has a voice, too, and I have to do the best I can to match it. Still, I manage to sneak a little of myself in where I can. If you know me really well, you'll notice the way I word things in all my stories. Sometimes my voice is hard to spot, but it's always there.

YOUR CHECKLIST FOR BETTER VOICE

To get a sense of how strong your voice is now, take a piece of your own writing that you really like, something that represents your best work, and answer the questions on the checklist below.

You know your writing has strong voice when:

Your readers can tell you care about your topic. Why did you pick your topic? Why is it important to you? Where in your writing will your readers be able to see how much you care about it?

—————————————————————————————

Your writing is filled with strong feelings and honest statements. What are your strongest feelings in this piece? Where do you express those feelings? Are you really being honest? Where does your honesty come through?

—————————————————————————————

Your writing is individual and authentic. Does the writing sound like you? Are you being yourself? What parts of the piece sound like only you could have written them?

—————————————————————————————

Your writing displays a well-defined personality. What parts of your personality come through in this piece? Where do those parts show up? What will readers think they know about who you are?

—————————————————————————————

Your writing has an appropriate tone for your purpose and your audience. Are you addressing your readers in a way that will make them feel honored and respected? Is it possible that anything you've written could offend your readers or otherwise discourage them from reading?

—————————————————————————————

You can do a lot to improve your voice by concentrating on the first two items in this checklist. For most of us, our writing comes alive when have topics we care about and when we communicate our feelings about them accurately and honestly.

SOMETHING WORTH CARING ABOUT

As you can imagine, I read a lot of kids' writing. Most of it is writing kids do in school. And most of it has very little voice. As I scan paper after paper, I often get the feeling that these young writers don't care about what they're doing. Most seem to write just to finish the assignments their teachers give them and to get a grade.

Writing is hard. It takes effort to do it well. And few of us feel like putting in that effort when we're writing about things we don't care about. When we're not invested in our topics, we don't invest much of ourselves into writing about them. In school, kids are often assigned topics that don't interest them. And this is one reason so much school writing lacks voice.

What's the connection between voice and interesting topics? Think about the topic I'm working on now. If I didn't care about voice—if I didn't think it was the most important quality in writing—I wouldn't put this much effort into explaining it to you. This chapter would be very short. I wouldn't include many details. Nor would I offer examples from my own experience.

Each of these things is an opportunity for me to express my voice as a writer. And with each expression, my voice improves and my writing gets a little more interesting. My writing gets more interesting because I'm interested in it in the first place. If I didn't care about the topic, I probably wouldn't care what I wrote about it—or if I even wrote about it at all.

Read Like a Writer:

The Fingerprint of the Author

One of my favorite authors is a man named William Kennedy. I think I've read all of his books. Every time he comes out with a new one, I pick it up as quickly as I can. As soon as I crack the binding and begin to read the first page, I get a feeling I've read the book before. I haven't, of course. But I can sense something about the writing that feels familiar. It's in the choice of the words and the snap of the sentences. It's in the characters and the way they inhabit their circumstances. It's in the setting, the plot, the issues and ideas Kennedy explores. What is "it"? Sometimes we call it the fingerprint of the author. Like a human fingerprint, it's made up of many different elements that, when taken together, form a unique way of identifying a text as being written by a specific person. All great authors leave their fingerprints behind. Can you raise them the books you read and solve the mystery of the author's voice?

Sometimes I have to write about things I'm not interested in. In the world of professional writing, many topics are assigned. But even though I can't choose my topic, I can still choose what I write about it. It's in this set of choices that I find ways to express my voice as a writer.

When I'm writing about something I don't care about, I try to imagine why my readers would care. And then I start to care about that. This often replaces the inspiration I would normally get from a topic I like. It also gets me focused on the reader instead of on myself—something that also improves my effort.

Miss Margot says

I have to write about stuff I don't care about all the time. It's my job. Sometimes, when you read my first draft, you can tell I'm bored or uninterested. So before I revise, I read the piece over and look for one thing in it that I can care about. That helps me care more about the subject as a whole. If I don't find anything in the story, I think about the commitment I've made to the person who is hiring me and how I never want to let my clients down. If that doesn't do the trick, I think about the pride I take in my work, and the fact that I hate doing a bad job on anything. Either way, I'm sort of tricking myself into becoming more invested in the story so I can turn out a better finished project. You might have to do something like this in school, too, from time to time.

A big part of why I write has to do with why people read. I know that readers want a good experience and that this means providing them with writing that is interesting and energetic—writing with strong voice. I think a lot about who I'm writing for and how they'll react to each word, phrase, and sentence I compose.

The way I look at it, some topics aren't worth caring about, but all readers are. There's something powerful for me in knowing that I'm talking to real people through my writing. I don't want to disappoint them. I don't want them to discover, through my flat and boring voice, that I didn't respect them enough to make what I wrote worth the time and effort they made to read it.

WHAT A DIFFERENCE A VOICE MAKES

If we want to see how voice makes writing better, all we have to do is look at two pieces on the same topic—one with weak voice, the other with strong voice. In the following examples, two students from the same class chose to write about the same thing: getting scared. As you might expect, their pieces have obvious similarities. But they ended up with dramatically different results.

Getting Scared

Getting scared is okay, I guess. Sometimes it's bad but sometimes it isn't. It just depends.

Movies are scary. TV shows can be scary, too. I think movies are scarier in the theater because it's so dark. We can turn the lights off when we watch TV but it still isn't as dark as in the movies.

One time I got really scared when I had a dream. I can't remember what happened in the dream but when I woke up I thought the dream was still going. Then my mom came into my room.

I don't try to scare people because I don't think it's nice. My little brother tried to sneak up on our cat while it was eating dinner and our cat turned around and scratched his arm. He ran to my mom. But she said it was his fault for bothering the cat at dinner time.

This is what I think about getting scared.

This first piece is just plain boring. It has no life, no energy, no voice. It could have been written by anyone. We don't get any sense at all about the personality of the writer. (No one could be as dull as the writing in this piece.) About all we can tell is that she's probably bored with the topic. But notice how different the second piece is.

The Attack of My Older Brother

I absolutely hate being scared. Especially when the person doing the scaring is my older brother. He's always trying to freak me out and that makes me mad. Just thinking about it drives me crazy.

My older brother has tried to scare me lots of times, lots of ways, in lots of different situations. I think one of the worst times was when I got home from school and expected to find him waiting for me or watching television. But my brother wasn't home, so I yelled for my dad outside. My dad wasn't home either. This was weird. There was always someone home after school. But now I was alone.

I walked all over the house, opening doors, looking in rooms, calling for other members of my family. Nothing. Then, right when I was walking into my brother's room, boom! He jumped out of the closet. I screamed and ran out into the hall. I was really frightened. I'll never forget the attack of my older brother. It will scar me for life.

My brother tries to scare me all the time. It's so annoying. For example, I'll be coming up from the basement with a huge load of laundry when all of a sudden he'll yell from the top of the stairs and drop sofa pillows on me. Another time, I was lying down on the floor in the TV room while we were all watching a scary movie. Just as something bad was about to happen, my brother grabbed both of my feet and made the same sound that the monster made in the movie. I nearly jumped out of my skin.

When it comes to scaring people, my brother is very talented. I think it's because he practices so much. He's always trying to scare somebody or something. If it's not me, or one of my sisters, he tries to scare our dog. (This doesn't work very well. Our dog is pretty old.) The only person he never tries scaring is our oldest brother. I think he knows that what might happen next would be the scariest thing of all.

Are you in a similar situation? Do you live in fear like I do every waking moment? Let me give you some advice: Don't take it seriously. It might be scary, but don't let it get to you. That's the best cure. Even for the attack of my older brother.

As soon as we read the title of this piece, we sense something different. This piece is going to be fun and playful. Right away, we get the writer's strong feelings. The piece is full of energy and humor. In the end, the writer can even laugh at herself a bit. I get the sense that this writer is a relatively mature person, even though she probably isn't very old. I like the way she talks directly to her audience. Best of all, I can tell she put some effort into this piece. Even though she had the same topic as the first writer, she worked hard to make it her own and to come up with interesting things to share with her readers.

ONCE MORE WITH FEELING

A bandleader rehearses a group on a new tune. The band plays through the piece several times. Each time they get better. But they never get good enough. The musicians know the notes and rhythms, but the music sounds dull and uninspiring, and the bandleader isn't satisfied. "Okay, let's try it once more with feeling," he says. And that makes all the difference.

The old expression, "once more with feeling," says as much about writing as it does about music. Without feeling, our pieces are dull. Emotions bring our writing to life in the minds and hearts of our readers.

But what is the connection between writing with strong feelings and developing a strong writer's voice? Imagine a room full of people sitting in chairs, each with the same blank expression. Nobody's smiling, nobody's frowning, everyone's just sitting there, staring into space with the same dull look on their faces. Which of these people would you most like to talk to? Probably none of them. And even if you had to pick, would it make any difference which person you chose? Each seems equally uninteresting.

This is what it's like for readers when they encounter writing that lacks emotion. Word after word, sentence after sentence, paragraph after paragraph, it all just seems boring. Even worse is the fact that one writer's boring work sounds a lot like every other writer's boring work. In a world of feelingless writing, all writing feels the same.

But that's not what you want when you sit down to write. You want your writing to be as unique as you are. The goal of improving your writer's voice is all about making your writing more individual, more personal, more like you. This is the key to making people want to read what you write. And often, a great way to do that is to put more feeling into it.

Miss Margot says

People often tell me they like the pieces I write where I express my true feelings—especially the ones where I'm really upset or excited, the ones I care about most. People tell me things like, "I can hear you saying that," or "I could just imagine your face when you wrote that." That's because there's more of me in those pieces than in any others I write.

I'M GETTING THE FEELING...

Bringing emotion to your writing is more than just telling people how you feel, it's about showing it. Think back to the two pieces about getting scared. The first writer mentions things that are scary but her writing is still dull and uninteresting. It's as though she doesn't really feel the way she says she does. By contrast, the second writer displays a wide range of emotions. When she gets scared, we feel it. But we also feel other things, too, like frustration and laughter. With regard to emotions, what's the difference between these two pieces?

Remember back in "Chapter 3: Better Ideas," when we talked about using "showing" details to make your writing more descriptive? That's the difference. In the first piece, the writer is just telling us about getting scared but not showing us anything:

> One time I got really scared when I had a dream. I can't remember what happened in the dream but when I woke up I thought the dream was still going. Then my mom came into my room.

But in the second piece, the writer shows us with great descriptive details:

> I walked all over the house, opening doors, looking in rooms, calling for other members of my family. Nothing. Then, right when I was walking into my brother's room, boom! He jumped out of the closet. I screamed and ran out into the hall. I was really frightened. I'll never forget the attack of my older brother. It will scar me for life.

Almost every feeling we can have can be described using "showing" details. We can also use "showing" a different way to convey emotion. Take a look at this:

> Nobody knew what went on in the old house on the hill. No one had gone in or come out in years. The roof was sagging, the windows were cracked, and thick cobwebs filled the corners under the eaves. Though none of us had ever been inside, we imagined dark and dusty rooms overrun with rats and roaches.

We don't have to say that the house was scary, or that someone was scared by it, to bring scary feelings into our writing. We can use descriptive "showing" details to set a mood for the reader.

THE PRESENCE OF THE AUTHOR

As readers read your writing, they experience a variety of emotions. Naturally, these feelings are associated with what you've written, but they're also associated with what they imagine about you as the writer. For example, when I get to a suspenseful part of a Harry Potter book, I know that J. K. Rowling is back there, somewhere, manipulating my emotions. I may not be able to tell what she's doing, but I know she's doing something because I sense the presence of the author.

Read Like a Writer:

Who's Pulling the Strings?

The next time you find yourself getting caught up in a great part of a great book, see if you can pull back just enough to figure out what's going on behind the scenes. For example, if you're scared, try to pinpoint the actual words and phrases that scare you. If you're sad, ask yourself what parts are getting you down. How is the author making you feel the way you're feeling? If you can answer this question (or even just remember to ask it), you'll be that much closer to learning how to get your own readers to feel the way you want them to feel.

Thinking back again to those two pieces about being scared, in which one does the author have more presence? Obviously, it's the second one. As you read through the piece, you can find several points where she's trying to make you feel something. You may or may not feel exactly what the author wants you to feel. But at least you can feel the author trying to stir your emotions.

Strengthening your voice strengthens your presence in a piece of writing. When your writing sparkles with strong feelings, your readers know you're right there with them, peeking over their shoulder as they turn the pages.

I had a teacher in college who had a great way of describing this connection between reader and writer. Dr. Canedo said that you knew you were reading a great book when, after you finished the final page, you wanted to jump up and shake the writer's hand. That's how you want your readers to feel. Just remember that, in order for your readers to want to shake your hand, they first have to know you're there.

Miss Margot says

A strong voice is especially important in persuasive writing. This is because you want your readers to think and act the way you do. And the best way to make that happen is to make an emotional appeal. Sure, you need good facts and solid logic, but you also need to present this information in a way that makes people connect with you as a person they can trust. If your readers like you and can identify with you in some way, you've got a better chance of getting them to think and do what you want.

ONLY YOU

If you haven't had this experience yet in your life, you certainly will sooner or later. It happens to me most often when I'm reading something someone has sent me in an e-mail or when I'm surfing the Internet. All of a sudden, I get the feeling I know who the author is, even though nobody's name is on the piece. Something about the way the writing feels tips me off. And even if I don't know what that is, I know I'm right because only one person could have written it.

When readers can correctly identify you as the author of a piece of writing, you know your voice is coming through loud and clear. At first, this might seem impossible. But if you think about some of the authors you read regularly, you'll get a better sense of how it works.

Think about books that come in a series like the Lemony Snicket books, for example. Each one is written in the same distinctive style with long sentences and some unusual vocabulary. Each one deals with similar ideas, similar characters, similar situations. I'll bet after reading just a couple of Lemony Snicket books you could identify any of the others as being written by the same author.

Most authors don't write series books. And yet, if you've read enough of their work, you can still discover the patterns that make their writing unique. Your writing will have patterns, too, even if you're not sure what they are yet. Readers who read your work regularly will come to recognize these patterns as part of your voice, and when they hear it, they'll know it's you.

YOUR WRITING, YOUR CHOICE

Way back at the beginning of this chapter, I said that voice is choice. The patterns in your writing that make up your voice come from the choices you make as a writer. Some writers choose the same topics and ideas over and over. Some writers choose the same words and styles of sentences. Some writers choose the same forms and organizational structures. Some writers create characters, settings, and situations with strong similarities. The choices you make—about what to write, how to write, why to write—have a degree of consistency because you're the only person making them.

As a unique person in the world, you make unique choices as a writer. If you produce enough writing, and if you pay attention to the choices you make, you'll eventually figure out what makes your writing unique to you. This is a long process that happens over many years. Making that process even more challenging is the fact that as the years go by, you'll be changing, too. As you mature, so will your voice as a writer.

Read Like a Writer:

The Song Remains the Same

This time I'm going to challenge you to read yourself. You may not be able to do this easily, but it's worth a try because it's so interesting. While there are many aspects of our writer's voice that change as we grow up, some will always be the same. Don't believe me? Try to find something you wrote several years ago. If you're thirteen or fourteen now, for example, ask your parents if they saved anything you wrote when you were nine or ten. I'll bet you'll find some striking similarities with how you write today. I've done this with my own writing (from as far back as twenty or thirty years ago!) and discovered that in many ways I haven't changed at all. It's a little weird; sort of like meeting a younger version of yourself. But it's also fascinating and, in terms of understanding your writer's voice, extremely valuable.

There's nothing more interesting than taking out a piece you wrote in the past and comparing it with a piece you've written in the present. Even if your subject is not yourself, a piece of writing can be an amazingly accurate reflection of who you were then and how you've changed to become who you are now.

Whenever you write, you leave a little of yourself behind. That's a good thing because it means that no one else can write exactly the same way you do. As your readers come to appreciate you as a writer, they'll want to read more of your work. The more they read, the more they'll appreciate the experience of reading something only you could have written.

BE A WRITER LIKE DANIEL WALLACE

Daniel Wallace is the author of three novels, Big Fish *(1998),* Ray in Reverse *(2000) and* The Watermelon King *(2003). His stories have been published far and wide in many magazines and anthologies, including The Yale Review, The Massachusetts Review, Shenandoah and Glimmer Train, and his illustrated work has appeared in the L.A. Times and Vanity Fair.* Big Fish *has been translated into 18 languages and was adapted for film by Tim Burton and John August.*

Q WHAT KIND OF WRITER ARE YOU?

A I write everything I can—articles, screenplays, directions—but mostly I write novels and short stories. My goal is to create something unique, something that's never been seen in the world before. I like to write about myths and magic.

Q WHY DO YOU WRITE?

A I love it. I love everything about it. Creating, working alone, the dress code, walking up the stairs to go to my office. I don't believe I have anything important to say, but sometimes something important slips out. I love it when that happens.

Q

WHAT MADE YOU WANT TO BE A WRITER?

I honestly don't know.

A

Q

WHAT ADVICE WOULD YOU GIVE TO A FELLOW WRITER WHO WAS JUST STARTING OUT?

Read. Write. Then read and write some more. Re-write what you've written. Write something and put it away for a month. Don't think about it. Then go back and look at it again. Then either throw it away or re-write it. Then show it to the world.

A

PERSON-ALITY

What makes a person the person they are? If we were in science class, we might say it has something to do with chromosomes and chemical reactions. But we're not in science class, so we'll have to look for something simpler.

When people read your writing, they can't help but read you, too. They know the piece was written by someone, and as they read, they start to think about who that someone is. Even if they don't know your name, they may feel like they're getting to know you through your writing.

In reality, they may not know much about you at all, but by reading your work, they may get to know your personality as a writer. And that's what makes a person the person they are—person-ality.

The simplest way to think about voice in writing is to think of it as personality. Your personality is the set of non-physical qualities (or traits as they are sometimes called) that make you you. Most of these qualities have to do with emotional things like how you feel most of the time, how you respond to things that happen to you, and how you interact with other people and the world. Every person has a personality. And every time we write, some of our personality comes through.

Ideally, if we're writing well, and our voice is strong, our writing will reflect who we are. What our readers will notice is that our work has some of the same personality traits we do. For example, if you're a very serious person, your readers might be able to detect your seriousness when you take on certain topics.

Read Like a Writer:

The Person Behind the Words

Sometimes, when we're talking about voice, we talk about "the person behind the words." When we use this expression, we're referring to who we think a writer is, based on what that writer has written. But it's not really the person behind the words that we see, it's the person-ality behind the words. So how would you describe the personality of your favorite author based on what you've read of his or her work?

GETTING TO KNOW YOU

One way to improve your voice is to put more of your personality into your writing. But before you can do that, you have to think a bit about what your personality is. This is not easy. Most of us never take time to step outside ourselves and get to know our own personalities. We just live with them.

Over the years, I've learned a few things about my own personality, some of which have found their way into my writing. For example, I'm a casual, informal person. I don't like it when people are stuffy or pretentious. So when I write, I try to stay away from big words or fancy ideas my readers might not understand. I try to write the way I talk when I'm talking to people in my normal everyday life. At times I don't use complete sentences, I favor contractions, and once in a while I even use slang. All of these things help transfer the casual, informal part of my personality to the printed page.

Two other personality traits that come through in my writing have to do with how much I like explaining things and how much I like to give advice. At times, these are good for my writing because they help me provide detailed explanations and thoughtful recommendations my readers find valuable. But these parts of who I am also have a dark side that can make my writing worse: Sometimes I explain too much and nobody wants to hear it. At other times, my advice-giving makes me sound overly critical, judgmental, or even arrogant. Nobody likes to be talked to that way either.

As you think more about your own personality, ask yourself how certain traits of yours show up in your writing. If you're a funny person, will your readers recognize your sense of humor? If you're a caring person, how does this part of you show up in what you write? Getting to know yourself this way will help you get to know your voice as a writer. And once you get to know your voice, your readers will have a better way of getting to know you.

THE BALANCING ACT

Up to this point, our discussion of voice has been all about you—who you are, how you feel, what you think, and so on. But writing isn't just about you. There's another person involved and that's the reader. Just as you have a need to express yourself, your reader needs something, too: it may be information; it may be entertainment; it may be a connection with another person who thinks and feels the same way. But no matter what it is, part of being a better writer is learning how to provide it.

Voice is about projecting your personality onto the page through words. But that's not all it's about. The true art of expressing your voice as a writer involves balancing your need to express yourself with your readers' expectations of how they want to be addressed. Often, this means adjusting your voice, changing it just a bit, to make it appropriate for your purpose and your audience.

For example, you have a way of acting with your friends when you're just hanging out. You have another way of acting when you're in class at school. You probably act a little differently when you're at home with your family. And if you went out to a fancy dinner or to church or to some other formal event, you might act just a little differently in these situations, too. You're still the same person, but you change the way you act as your situation changes. Why? Because you know what's appropriate for different purposes and different audiences. The same thing is true for writing.

Because I'm a casual person who likes to write with a casual tone, I often have to change my voice a bit for situations where more formality is required. For example, I communicate all the time through e-mail to my business clients. After we've worked together for a while, I may be able to write to them in a casual way, but at first I have to be relatively formal because this is what my audience expects when it comes to business communication.

Miss Margot says

I have different voices for different audiences. When I write love advice columns, I try to sound like your smarter older sister, someone who really cares about you, and who knows what she's talking about because she's been there herself. When I write about housing, I try to sound like an authority. When I write personality profiles, I try to sound like a person meeting someone for the first time. But no matter who I try to sound like, you can always tell it's me writing.

For most of us, changing the way we interact with people comes naturally when we're with them in person. We know how to change our tone, our words, our body language, and a million other things, often without even thinking about it. But it's different when we interact with imaginary readers on paper because there's no one else sitting with us when we write.

Using the wrong voice with your readers can be a disaster. Imagine how you'd come across if you talked the same way in the principal's office as you talk with your friends at the mall. In person, you'd never make this mistake. But in writing, we make it all the time. When this happens, we risk offending our audience, and when people are offended, they tend to withdraw or get angry. Neither of these reactions will help anyone like your writing—or you!

TIP:

Have you ever had to write a letter of apology to someone? How about a letter of condolence after someone has died? A thank you letter? A letter to a pen pal? Wouldn't you have to use a slightly different voice for each of these kinds of writing? Letters are great for learning about voice. In fact, they're probably better than any other form of writing we know. Why do you suppose that is? If you think it has something to do with audience, you're absolutely right. In no other form of writing do we think so carefully about the people we're writing to. In most cases, we don't even think to start a letter if we don't have a specific reader in mind. This strong sense of audience guides our voice as we write. But you can hone your voice even when you're not writing letters. Just make it a habit to write as though you were writing to one specific person, someone who represents the larger audience reading your work.

In my twenties, when I was just starting out as a professional writer, I often made mistakes with voice, especially in business situations. Fortunately, I never offended anyone too horribly, or caused any serious problems, but I did lose many of my readers, mostly because they didn't take me seriously. I kept thinking I was right to write in the way that made me most comfortable—the casual, informal way that most closely matched my personality. I didn't realize that many readers weren't comfortable reading it (or if I did, I didn't care). So in order to communicate more effectively in business, I had to change my attitude and change my voice.

To make those changes, I did something simple: I began to imagine myself talking to my readers in a formal business situation. Sometimes I would see myself making a presentation or giving a speech. At other times, I would see myself talking to someone in an office or leading a meeting with a small group around a conference table. It didn't matter what image I came up with. As long as someone representing my audience was in it, and I could conjure up the right real-life situation, I was able to develop an appropriate voice.

What I'm talking about here just comes down to respect. You have to respect yourself, of course; you have to be who you are. But you also have to interact with your audience in a way that honors who they are. In order to read your writing, readers have to make an investment of time, energy, and effort. Respect that investment by addressing them in a voice that acknowledges the way they want to be treated and the reason they are reading your work. If you can learn to do that—if you can learn to master the balancing act of voice—you'll be doing more to make yourself a better writer than almost anything else.

CHAPTER SIX
Better Words

TEN THINGS YOU NEED TO KNOW
EVEN IF YOU DON'T READ THIS CHAPTER

1. If you're going to focus on one type of word, pick verbs. Nothing will improve your writing more than improving the verbs you use.

2. A strong verb is one that has the meaning of an adverb inside it; it's a verb that not only communicates an action but also tells the reader how that action is performed.

3. Most writing books will tell you that the passive voice is bad. But it has its place, especially when you want to hide the identity of the person or persons performing an action.

4. Many people will tell you to write like you talk. But a better approach is to draft like you talk. Get your ideas down as quickly and as easily as possible. Then go back later in revision and improve your word choice.

5. Most of the things you'll learn about improving your word choice will be about making your language more specific and precise.

6. Big words may seem impressive when other people use them, but small words are often more appropriate and more effective.

7. For a great word choice exercise, try writing a piece without using a certain letter of the alphabet (like "e" or "a") or a certain common word (like "the" or "and").

8. Individual words can be interesting, but more often it's how we group words together in unusual phrases that gets our readers' attention.

9. Improving your word choice is not about finding fancy words. It's about finding words that work—language that reaches readers in a way that sounds true to the writer who writes it.

10. When you're writing for your friends, it's fine to use casual language. But when you're writing for adults, you may have to shift your language into a higher gear, and write more formally, if you want to be taken seriously.

STICKS AND STONES

"Sticks and stones may break my bones but words will never hurt me." That may be true on the playground, but here at my desk, under deadline pressure and behind as usual, the fact that I can't find the words I need is definitely a painful experience.

Most people who know me would say I have a large vocabulary. They'd probably also say I talk a lot, read a lot, love language, and that I'm rarely at a loss for words—unless I'm writing. Anyone who knows how I write knows that most of what I do isn't writing, it's rewriting. I labor endlessly over lists of synonyms. I try one turn of phrase and then another—writing, erasing, and writing again until I sometimes forget what I wanted to say in the first place. I'm always looking for better words even when the ones I have are probably good enough.

As ridiculous as it sounds, I like to think of myself as a word warrior, fighting for truth and clarity, wielding language like a sword. But I'm really more of a word worrier instead. I'm always asking questions like: Does this make sense? Will my readers understand me? Is there a better way to say this? I like to think that my word worrying is productive, that the effort I put in really does make my writing better. But that isn't always the case. Sometimes, while searching for the best way to express myself, I end up creating more problems than I solve.

Take my last book, for example. I must have read and revised every sentence ten times. Then I sent it out to a group of friends over e-mail. Almost instantly, I had a mountain of suggestions in my inbox for better ways to say things. I had spent months carefully constructing my sentences, packing them with the best words I could find, only to discover that, in just a few minutes, several of my friends came up with even better ones.

Ouch. That hurts. Sticks and stones would be less painful.

TIP:

It's one thing when people tell you your writing could be better. It's another thing entirely when they change your words. And yet, this is exactly what so many people like to do when they give you feedback. How do I deal with it? By remembering that feedback is more about the person giving it than the person getting it. When someone tells me there's a better way to say something, I know that what they're really saying is that that's how they'd say it if they were the author. But they're not; I am. So I get to decide—at least until my editors and publisher overrule me. Since I know that the feedback I get from people is really about them and how they feel, I don't have to let it bother me. I can use what I find helpful and ignore what I don't.

WHY ARE WORDS SO HARD TO WORK WITH?

Working with words should be the easiest part of writing. After all, we know thousands of them, we use them every day, we only have to deal with them one at a time, and most of them are short. With only the slightest effort, words should fly from our fingers and arrange themselves in perfect order on the page. But they don't. And even the best writers can't explain why.

Deep inside each of us there has to be some brain-to-body process we use to find words for our ideas. And since our brains and our bodies are more alike than they are different, that process should be more or less the same for every writer. But how that process works is one of the great mysteries of our craft. Or maybe it's not a mystery. Maybe it's a puzzle. Or a riddle. Or a conundrum. Or an enigma. Or any of a half dozen other words I just looked up in my favorite online thesaurus.

Aye, there's the rub: We've got so many words to choose from, we don't know which ones to choose.

Scientists estimate that the average kindergartener knows 10,000 words. A high schooler, 60,000. A well-educated adult, 120,000. People in specialized professions, like doctors and lawyers, may have vocabularies even larger than that. And this isn't nearly all the words there are. Some large English-language dictionaries have half a million words in them.

Worst of all is the fact that we have no way of knowing if our readers know the same words we do. Writing is communication. But we don't communicate very well when we use words our readers don't understand. And things get even crazier when we start using words we don't understand.

Words are tricky. The same ones mean different things to different people. They change their meanings depending on how they're used. Old ones die out. New ones are invented every day. And even the most respected dictionaries sometimes disagree about what certain words mean.

Words: Can't write with 'em, can't write without 'em.

WORDS TO DESCRIBE WORDS

One thing we can be sure of is that readers appreciate well-chosen words. The quality of a writer's language is one of the first things people notice. But what is it exactly that they're noticing? Here are five important things:

- **Strong verbs that show how actions are performed.** Did you know that some verbs are stronger than others? I didn't either until I started studying writing. Take a verb like "run," for example. It doesn't give us nearly as much information as the verb "sprint." When we read that someone sprinted away, we know they ran but we also know they ran very quickly. Verbs that include this extra information are said to be stronger—and thus more highly valued—than those that don't.

- **Words that make ideas more specific.** In general, it's better to be specific than it is to be general. You've got an idea in your head. You want to get it down on paper so it can find its way into someone else's head. The more specific your language, the more likely it is that your readers will receive the same message you send.

- **Groups of words that readers find meaningful and memorable.** Readers may read words one at a time, but they tend to be more impressed when writers arrange them in small groups. For the most part, we don't think much about coming up with surprising combinations of words. But a well-crafted turn of phrase here and there is all it takes to turn basic writing into better writing—and better writing is more likely to be remembered by our readers.

- **"Just right" words used in just the right way.** There's a part of effective word choice that some people call "usage." To use words effectively, we not only have to know their definitions, we also have to be aware of the common situations, or contexts, in which they are used. Good usage takes a long time to develop. Most people pick it up by listening to good speakers and by reading good writers.

- **Appropriate language for purpose and audience.** Everyone knows there are words and phrases that shouldn't be used in some writing situations. People may say this is bad language, or that you're a bad person for using it, but the simplest truth is that it's just bad writing because inappropriate language makes it hard for people to understand your ideas.

Words are everywhere. We can hardly go through a minute of our lives without seeing them, saying them, hearing them, or thinking about them. But writing them is a little different, especially when we're trying to write well. Writing isn't about using words; it's about choosing words. And because there are so many words to choose from, and so many different ways to string them together, hunting for the best ones is sometimes a tedious task. But it can also be incredibly satisfying.

There's a feeling we get when we find the perfect words to express an idea. It's like the feeling of solving a puzzle, winning a game, or guessing the number of marbles in a huge glass jar. Better still is the feeling we get when our readers tell us they thought our words were perfect, too. Beautifully crafted language is both meaningful and magical. Like saying a prayer or making a wish, putting the right words together in just the right way can make amazing things happen.

 # YOUR CHECKLIST FOR BETTER WORDS

Because the words we use are so much a part of who we are, it can be difficult to discover how we need to improve in this aspect of our writing. To raise our awareness, it's helpful to consider some criteria for effective word choice, along with a few key questions we can ask ourselves when we assess our work.

You know you're doing a great job with words when your writing has:

Strong verbs that show how actions are performed. Where have you used strong verbs? How do they show readers how actions are performed? What makes them more effective than the weak verbs and modifiers they are replacing?

Words that make ideas more specific. Where is your language most specific? How do these places differ from places where your language is more general? Where you've chosen more specific language, how do you know you understand the exact meanings of the words you're using?

Groups of words readers find meaningful and memorable. Where do you find groups of words that are especially meaningful and memorable? What makes these phrases so effective? Are there similarities or patterns in these groups of words that you can use as strategies to improve other parts of your writing?

"Just right" words used in just the right way. Where have you reworded parts of sentences to make them more effective? Where have you been able to make your writing more efficient by removing words that were redundant or otherwise unnecessary? Where have you been able to substitute one or two high-quality words for longer strings of less effective words? Have you checked the meanings of words you're unsure of so you know you're using them correctly?

Appropriate language for purpose and audience. Who is your audience? Why are you writing to them? How do they want to be addressed? How do they speak and write? What expectations do they have of you in terms of the language you will use and how you will address them? Have you used any words that your readers may find offensive?

The way to approach improving your use of words is very gradually, perhaps even one word at a time. Often, I'm happy if I can fix a single phrase in a piece. Concentrating on small victories in the war on words has had two big advantages for me: it keeps me from going crazy looking for every nitpicky little problem; and it helps me gain confidence in my ability to find and fix the common errors I make on a regular basis.

WHERE THE ACTION IS

Verbs are where the action is—literally and figuratively. As you've probably been told a thousand times, verbs are the action words in a sentence. When I go to the store, "going" is the action and "go" is the verb. That's the literal part of the equation. It's easy to understand but it's not going to help you become a better writer no matter how many "find the verb" worksheets your teachers ask you to fill out.

More valuable is the notion that verbs are the engines of our sentences. Nothing energizes writing more than high-powered verbs; no other type of word commands a reader's attention so effectively. Verbs make the message move. And using them well will definitely make you a better writer.

ARE YOUR VERBS AS STRONG AS THEY CAN BE?

Year after year when I was in school, and even for many years thereafter, teachers and other writing advisors told me I needed to use strong
verbs. But nobody ever told me what a strong verb was, why we used
the word "strong" to describe them, or how to exchange them for the
weak verbs I was apparently foisting on my readers.

As I mentioned in the previous section, writing is full of mysteries.
Some are truly unknowable, like the way words travel from our brain
to our fingers to the page. But many others are not. And so it is with
the "mystery" of the strong verb.

Because you shouldn't have to go through the many years of frustration
I did trying to figure this one out, here's the skinny on strong verbs:

- **What is a strong verb?** A strong verb is one that has the meaning
  of an adverb inside it. It's a verb that not only communicates an
  action but also tells the reader how that action is performed. An
  adverb, as you may recall from many a boring grammar lesson, is
  a word that modifies a verb. Many of them end in "ly." So let's say
  you write the following sentence: "The man walked leisurely down
  the street." In this case, "walked" is the verb and "leisurely" is the
  adverb that modifies it; "leisurely" tells you how the man walked.
  But instead, you could write this sentence: "The man ambled down
  the street." The verb "ambled" means "walked leisurely." It conveys
  the meaning of the weak verb "walked" and the meaning of the
  adverb "leisurely" at the same time.

- **Why do we use the term "strong" to describe them?** When
  you write "ambled" instead of "walked leisurely," you're using one
  word to do the work of two. That's what makes one verb stronger
  than another. By including in a single word both the action and
  how that action is performed, strong verbs carry more information
  more efficiently than weak verbs do. Sometimes a strong verb can
  do the work of an entire phrase. For example, the meaning in this
  sentence: "The man walked down the street, showing off as though

he were trying to attract attention" is pretty much the same as the meaning in this sentence: "The man paraded down the street." In the first case, "showing off as though he were trying to attract attention" is what some people might call an "adverbial phrase" or a group of words that modifies a verb. In the second case, the strong verb "paraded" carries off the whole scene vividly by itself.

- **How do I put strong verbs into my writing?** Our teachers probably hope that strong verbs would jump right out of us during drafting. But that rarely happens for me. So I focus on strengthening verbs in revision. For the most part, when I draft, it's all I can do to get my ideas down. But as I re-read, I tell myself to be on the lookout for all the weak verbs I've left behind. When I spot one, I ask myself questions like these: "How could I make the verb I'm using more specific? How could I describe the way the action is being performed? Is there an adverb or adverbial phrase in the sentence I might be able to replace with a single strong verb?" Sometimes these questions jog my memory and an appropriate strong verb pops into my head. But when that doesn't happen, I go to an online thesaurus and look up synonyms for the weak verb I'm trying to improve. When I find a synonym that looks promising, I look up its meaning in an online dictionary to make sure I'm using it accurately.

Strong verbs don't have to be unusual verbs; strength is not a matter of obscurity, it's a matter of specificity. Ambling is a kind of walking. But so is pacing, striding, or marching. If we refer to what someone is doing simply as "walking," that's a general term. Using a stronger verb gives our readers a clearer, more specific picture of what's going on.

If you want a shorthand way of remembering what a strong verb is, try this: STRONG VERB = VERB + ADVERB. A strong verb is a single word that carries within it the meaning of a weak verb plus an adverb or adverbial phrase.

Read Like a Writer:

Looking for Strong Verbs

While it's important to understand how strong verbs work grammatically, it's much more useful to understand how they feel to your readers. Just about anything you read will have at least a few examples of strong verbs. Seek them out. When you find them, try to break them down. Take the strong verb and see if you can determine the weak-verb-plus-adverb combination that would mean the same thing.

THE DREADED PASSIVE VOICE

Another famous teacher term that haunted me throughout school and well into my early professional writing years was the "passive voice." I knew it had something to do with verbs and I knew it was bad. But that was all I knew. Like so many obscure grammar terms, this one really threw me. Turns out, it wasn't nearly as complicated as I thought.

Compare these two sentences:

1. Mr. G. I. Lovemoney purchased the winning lottery ticket. (Active Voice)

2. The winning lottery ticket was purchased by Mr. G. I. Lovemoney. (Passive Voice)

In sentence #1, the actor performing the action (Mr. Lovemoney) comes first. In sentence #2, the actor comes last. That's all there is to it. Now, why should you care about this? Actually, there are several very reasonable reasons.

In general, readers prefer active voice sentences because:

- **Active voice sentences order things in the way most readers expect.** There's a natural way we learn to put sentences together in English. Grammar people call it "Subject-Verb-Object." For example, "I shot the sheriff, but I did not shoot the deputy." ("I" is the subject, "shot" is the verb, "sheriff" is the object—and nobody worries about the deputy because he didn't get shot!) This sounds normal. By contrast, the following passive voice construction sounds strange: "The sheriff was shot by me, but the deputy was not shot by me." Not only is this a poor way to say something, it would never become a hit song.

- **Active voice sentences are easier to remember.** If the police who have captured me need to remember my confession, they'll have an easier time if I express it in the active voice. Of course, if I want to confuse them in the hope that they will let me go, the passive voice might be a better strategy.

- **Active voice sentences are shorter.** If I'm filling out a form to make my confession, I can fit more of the gruesome details of my crime into the small space allowed. If I use the passive voice, I won't have enough room to explain; I may fill out the form incorrectly, and my confession may be invalid.

- **Active voice sentences are less ambiguous.** Because the passive voice plays around with who is doing what, the resulting statement sometimes isn't clear. If I'm not careful, I may end up going to jail for the murders of both the sheriff and the deputy!

Most writing books will tell you that the passive voice is bad. I'm going to tell you that the active voice sounds more natural to your readers and that using it will help you stay true to your own natural way of writing. But I'm also going to tell you that there are occasionally interesting situations where the passive voice may be just what the doctor ordered.

In my twenties, I worked in the software industry. Because software is an international business, I often had to meet international businessmen. One time I was part of a group from our company that had to greet a team of Japanese executives at the airport. There were five of us and seven of them. When we met them at the gate, a comic and chaotic scene unfolded:

> For the next fifteen minutes, introductions were awkwardly made, hands were tentatively shaken, and uncertain bows were exchanged so haphazardly no one knew when to stop.

When I write this way, I'm using the passive voice deliberately—I don't want you to know who is doing what, I just want you to know what's being done. I also want you to feel the awkwardness of the situation. By using the passive voice, and leaving out the actors entirely, I keep your attention right where I want it: on a melee of over-politeness that looked more like some strange dance than a bunch of businessmen getting to know each other.

So the passive voice has its place. And that place usually turns up when you want to hide the identity of the person or persons performing an action. Of course, the best time to hide the identity of an actor is when he will end up in trouble if his identity is revealed. As the old saying goes, "When the passive voice is being used, blame is being avoided." Just don't be too eager to use the passive voice to obscure your own misdeeds. When we use it in talking about ourselves, it's a dead giveaway.

TIP:

The next time a teacher or anybody else uses a grammar term you don't understand, ask them to stop using it and to explain what they mean in normal everyday language. Almost everyone struggles with grammar. And while some of it is truly challenging, most of it isn't—until someone starts using unfamiliar terms that are not connected clearly to the concepts they represent (like the terms "active voice" and "passive voice", for example). Even the most complex language concepts can be discussed in simple language. So the next time someone wants you to learn something about grammar, ask them to explain it using words you understand and are comfortable with.

I KNOW EXACTLY WHAT YOU MEAN

Yesterday, I went out to lunch. The host seated me and gave me a menu. I looked it over briefly and then my waiter arrived. "Can I take your order?" he said cheerfully. "Yes," I promptly responded. "I'll have a large house salad with extra chicken, Italian dressing, and a Coke."

A few minutes later, my order arrived. The chicken and the dressing were on my salad, the Coke was not. How did the waiter know this was the way I wanted it? Why not put the Coke on the salad, too? Or serve the dressing in a glass with ice on the side?

Most people know what we're saying because of the context in which we say it. That's why my waiter knew I wanted my Coke in a glass and not in a bowl with my lettuce and tomatoes. And if for some reason he wasn't sure, all he would have had to do was ask me.

In our speaking and listening lives, we get used to being casual with words. Nothing wrong with that. But when we write something, we can't be there, staring over our readers' shoulders, ready to pop in with a clarifying remark every time we see a raised eyebrow or a confused look. This is why we often have to put forth an extra effort to choose words that say exactly what we mean.

TIP:

Many writing teachers and writing books will tell you to write like you talk. The problem with this advice is that most of us don't speak accurately or eloquently enough to meet our readers' expectations for clarity and quality. So my advice is to draft like you talk. Use your normal everyday vocabulary, and your natural way of speaking, to get your ideas down as quickly and as easily as possible. Then go back and revise your word choice later.

SOMETHING WE NEVER THINK ABOUT

We all have a tendency to think that communicating via the written word is a rather straightforward affair. A writer writes something, a reader reads it. It's a simple two-step process. But in reality it's not so simple, and it's certainly more than two steps. It's at least a four-step process, and all kinds of things can go wrong along the way.

Here's one way of looking at it: A writer thinks of an idea (Step 1) and then finds words to express that idea (Step 2); a reader reads the words (Step 3) and then interprets those words to understand what the writer means (Step 4). If all goes well, when the reader finishes interpreting, he'll have in his head the same idea the writer started with at the beginning. But it doesn't always work out that way.

There are three different places where the transaction between writer and reader can break down:

- **Between the writer's idea and the writer's words.** If the words I choose don't accurately reflect my idea, there's little chance that my message will be clear, even if my readers read carefully and understand what I've written.

- **Between the writer's words and the reader's reading.** The fact that I choose my words carefully is no guarantee my readers will bring the same level of care to their part of the deal. Readers make mistakes when they read. Sometimes they're not familiar with the vocabulary they encounter. Sometimes they just skip over stuff they're not interested in and miss something important.

- **Between the reader's reading and the reader's interpretation.** Even if I've chosen the right words, and my readers read them perfectly, the message could still get garbled if they don't interpret my language in the same way I did when I wrote it.

As I've mentioned before, there's no way to be sure our readers understand exactly what we mean. That's why writers have to work so hard to be as clear as they can be, and why carefully considering the words we use, even though this seems like a small part of writing, makes a huge difference in the quality and effectiveness of our work.

Miss Margot says

Ensuring clarity is a big role that editors play. Oh, sure, I have to think carefully about what words I want to use to convey the right message in the right way. But my editors are the final check-off point for that. They can get an even keener focus on what the reader needs because they don't have all those other ideas banging around in their heads like us writers do. If you find someone who can be a good editor for you, don't let them get away. Good editors are like gold!

LET'S GET SPECIFIC

Okay, enough theory. Let's get down to some practical tips for improving the exchange between reader and writer. Any hack with a typewriter can give you advice all day long about how to say certain things more effectively. In fact, there are entire books devoted to this aspect of word choice, each one filled with hundreds of wonderful suggestions. Personally, I've never found these books to be much help because I can't keep track of hundreds of wonderful suggestions while I'm writing. I figure I've got room in my brain for maybe six things at a time; if I have to deal with more than that I can't function.

Almost all the advice you'll ever read about choosing better words comes down to one incredibly important idea: Be specific. While you can't control how your reader reads your words, you can control the words your reader reads. If you make an effort to choose words that are as specific as possible, you'll have done everything you can to minimize the differences between what you mean and what your reader thinks you mean.

Here are six strategies for making your writing more specific:

- **Use strong verbs.** We've already gone over this one, but it bears repeating. Strengthening your verbs strengthens your writing. We don't use strong verbs just because they're cooler than weak ones. We use them because they tell the reader more about what's happening.

- **Use strong nouns.** If we have strong verbs, why can't we have strong nouns? If a strong verb is a verb with the meaning of an adverb inside it, a strong noun is one that includes the meaning of an adjective. For example, I could write something like this: "John was someone you could never figure out no matter how hard you tried; he was a puzzle without a solution." But this shorter, punchier sentence will get the same point across: "John was a conundrum."

- **Use meaningful modifiers.** We don't have to pack all the meaning into single nouns and verbs. It's fine to use adjectives and adverbs. But sometimes we throw them around carelessly. That's when we come up with sentences like these: "The food was unusually unique." (If something is unique, we already know it's unusual); "The ship was completely destroyed." (What's the difference between being destroyed and being completely destroyed?); and my all-time favorite, "You can visually see it!" (How else would you see it?) The point of using a modifier is to make an idea more specific without using redundant words. So when you use adjectives and adverbs, ask yourself these questions: Does the noun or verb I'm modifying already contain the meaning of the modifier I'm using? Does the modifier I'm using conflict in any way with the meaning of the noun or verb it's paired with? How does the modifier I'm using enhance the meaning of the noun or verb to make the sentence more specific?

- **Use the fewest words possible.** The more there is for readers to understand, the less likely they are to understand it. On the other hand, being specific sometimes requires a little extra language. So the rule of thumb is this: Say exactly what you need to say—but nothing more. Remove words that don't need to be there. This is not an easy thing to do. In fact, I find it so challenging that I leave it for a separate editing pass near the end of a writing project. (Want to know something really weird about this? I have never in my life not been able to remove a significant number of words from something I have finished writing. Even in pieces I think I have already picked to the bone, I still find that five to ten percent of the words don't need to be there. And the result is always a piece that is more interesting to read!)

- **Learn the meanings of words that are unusual to you.** This sounds like a dictionary strategy, not a writing strategy, doesn't it? But this is exactly what I do almost every time I sit down for some serious wordsmithing. I'll be looking over a sentence and all of a sudden an unusual word will occur to me. It's often a word I've heard before but one that is not a part of my everyday vocabulary. So I look it up. About half the time, it works perfectly. But even when it doesn't work, by looking it up, I learn a new word. Ironically, the larger my vocabulary gets, the more I feel inclined to look up words I'm unsure of. At this point in my writing career, I take pride in using words more accurately than I used to, and in knowing how different words are related through their definitions.

- **Learn to differentiate between synonyms.** Another thing I do when I'm revising for word choice is use an online thesaurus. I have a four-step process that looks like this: (Step 1) Find a word that says what I want to say but probably isn't the best word I could use; (Step 2) pop that word into my online thesaurus and see what other choices come up; (Step 3) sift through the list of synonyms for the word I really like; and then, before I use it in my writing, (Step 4) I look it up in a dictionary. This last step is crucial because all synonyms are not created equal. I can't just swap them, one for another, willy-nilly as though they all meant the same thing. If I don't understand the subtle differences between the synonyms my thesaurus offers me, I'm likely to make an embarrassing mistake.

Is this all you have to do to make your writing more specific? Hardly. As we've discussed, there are hundreds of different tricks for improving your word choice. But these six strategies cover a lot of ground. Even learning just one of them can make a difference in the quality of your work.

Miss Margot says

The other day I was working on a story about theft. In the process, I used the word "theft" so many times that I knew I was over-using it even before I finished drafting! So I went to the thesaurus and checked out a few other options. Most didn't work because they didn't "feel" right. When I read them in my sentences, they sounded funny or even wrong.
But I settled on a couple that worked. "Pilfering" was my favorite because it refers to the stealing of small items of little value—perfect for a part of my story where people were stealing small things. So watch those definitions when you're swapping synonyms.

A SMALL CAUTION ABOUT BIG WORDS

Big words are cool. And most people will think you're really smart when you use them. Your friends will be amazed, your teachers will be thrilled, and your parents' egos will swell with pride when they tell country club acquaintances that their little Johnny or Janey used "sesquipedalian" in a sentence yesterday on the way to T-ball practice.

Your readers, however, may be less enthusiastic.

Even though I've showed you strategies that will help you bring more interesting words into your writing, and even though I'm encouraging you to expand your vocabulary, I want you to temper your excitement for complex language with one simple truth: small words are often more effective than big ones.

Here's what I mean:

> Imagine employing an enforced rubric for text-based com-
> munication in which logograms of only a single syllable were
> permitted. How would this affect an author's ability to express
> concepts in a manner consistent with intention? Academic tradi-
> tion dictates that multi-syllable words are superior. But contrary
> to popular belief, single-syllable signifiers are exceedingly satis-
> factory. Their correctness is unassailable; their clarity without
> parallel. They are easier for readers to understand, and their use
> encourages us to produce texts more consistent with our own
> mode of natural verbal expression.

Now give this a quick read:

> What if there was a rule that said you had to use small words
> when you wrote? Could you still say what you had to say? We
> tend to think big words are worth more than small ones. But
> this is not true. Small words can do big things. They are clean,
> they are clear, they are strong, they are true. They help us write
> the way we talk, say what we mean, be who we are.

Both paragraphs say essentially the same thing. Which one sounds
better to you? Which one is clearer and easier to understand? Which
one would you like to read? Don't you think most other readers would
feel the same way?

The second paragraph is composed entirely of single syllable words.
Go ahead. Check it out. Not one multi-syllable word in there. You
won't find a set of smaller words than that. And yet, I think these
small words are extremely effective. That first paragraph might sound
erudite, but what if my readers don't know what "erudite" means? Why
bother with inscrutable displays of sesquipedalian prose when we can
say what we mean with words everyone knows?

Miss Margot says

One of my editors once busted my chops for using a big word when it wasn't really necessary. He said, "Don't use a dollar word when a dime word will do." So get out there and expand your vocabulary. Do crossword puzzles. Read dictionaries. Study Latin and Greek. Work hard to become more erudite! Just remember that big words won't necessarily get you a big readership.

ACTIVITY: BIG THOUGHTS, SMALL WORDS

I've had a blast over the years asking students to write entire essays (and poems!) using only single-syllable words. It's hard at first but soon you get the hang of it. Working with small words gives your writing a unique quality I've never been able to explain. You could just say the pieces sound cool when they're finished. And there's no doubt that writing such a piece is a great word choice workout. Give it a try. You'll be pleasantly surprised with the results.

MORE GREAT WORD CHOICE WORKOUTS

It's rare that I suggest exercises for the young writers I work with. Writing your own pieces is exercise enough. But when it comes to experiencing new word choice challenges, most of us—including yours truly—won't make the effort unless we're forced to do so. This means that in order to get better faster, we need to practice a little bit.

Below you'll find several suggestions for exercises that are both fun and good practice. Don't worry about whether you can do them all. Find one or two that interest you and really dig into them:

- **Write the way someone else talks.** This is hard but fascinating. It's an extremely useful skill to master because if you can learn to mimic the way other people speak, you can learn to mimic the way other writers write. Pick a friend. Pick an enemy. Pick a member of your family. Pick a character from a book, TV show, or movie. Choose a person you know well and try to get inside their head as they tell a story from their perspective.

- **Write a piece entirely in dialog.** This is sort of like writing a play, but don't put in any stage directions. Better yet, don't put in attributions either (no "he saids" and "she saids"). Tell a story with two or more people using only their words to get the message across. Make each character use a slightly different vocabulary. Help your readers keep track of who's talking by the words they use.

- **Write a piece with dialog but without using quotes.** There are some very talented writers who include dialog in their stories without enclosing it in quotation marks. The cool thing is that they write so well, and choose their words so carefully, they don't need to. Try this yourself. It's harder than it seems. The true test is giving your story to someone else and seeing if they can distinguish between the words of the narrator and the words of the characters.

- **Write a piece without any punctuation at all.** You may think this is easy because you do it all the time in e-mail or on your cell phone. But try writing something long and complicated without periods, capitals, and all those other good things. Once again, ask someone to read what you've written and to tell you where they get confused. Then, using only words, see if you can clear things up.

- **Write poems and songs that rhyme.** To write poetry and songs that rhyme, you have to choose your words carefully. A great way to make this even more interesting is to reject the first rhyming words that occur to you and dig a little deeper for rhymes that are not so obvious.

- **Write a piece without using a common word.** Pick a commonly used word like "the" or "and" and write an entire piece without using it. Handicapping yourself in this arbitrary way will force you out of your normal habits and into new and unfamiliar territory.

- **Write a piece without using a common letter.** This is similar to not using a particular word. But in this case, we write a piece without a particular letter. Choose to leave out "s", for example, and you can't use plurals or possessives very easily. Leave out "d" and you probably won't be able to use the past tense. Most challenging of all, however, is to leave out "e", the most commonly used letter in the English language.

Believe it or not, an entire book has been written without a single "e". That's right, thousands of words and not one of them uses the fifth letter of the alphabet. I can't imagine how the writer did this. It must have taken an incredible effort over a long period of time.

It took me nearly an hour to come up with the little e-less introduction below, and it has fewer than 150 words.

> On a pitch black January night, at an hour most inhabitants of Bolin Hollow might find unusual for such activity, a stout man with a small black bag limps slowly out of his yard, down a narrow path, past a row of shops, and into a thick wrap of fog. Unusual as it is, this nocturnal stroll is anything but unusual for Mr. Bostwick; his work brings him to many locations around this small town, and almost always at odd hours. Night is normal for Mr. B; in fact, many in his occupation find sunlight distracting—too much watching, too much human contact. But only fog follows him now, and though his gait is awkward—a motion similar to that of a man for whom drinking was a nightly pursuit—nothing will stop him from carrying out his duty.

I had to rework most of the sentences in this paragraph to stay away from words that had "e's" in them. To be honest, I'm still not sure I did it right. But if you find an "e" in there, do me a favor and don't tell me about it. I'm very proud of this little accomplishment.

BE A WRITER LIKE PETE ANDERSEN

Even as a high schooler Pete Andersen was a prolific writer cranking out plays and stories faster than his friends could read them. As an adult he has written for newspapers and magazines. He has also been a technical writer at Microsoft for many years. When he's not writing about computer software, he works on novels, screenplays, and essays. He's also a terrific e-mail buddy and he loves making lists.

Q WHAT KIND OF WRITER ARE YOU?

A

By day, I'm a technical writer, which means I write manuals which are supposed to help people use computer software.

But by night, I do the kind of writing that actually allows me to call myself a "writer." I write stories, screenplays, novels, whatever. I'm always working on about a dozen projects, and getting ideas for more all the time.

Q WHY DO YOU WRITE?

A

Because I go crazy when I don't.

I think every person finds many ways to express what they're feeling, through art, movement, relationships, whatever. For me, my main form of expression has always been writing. Thoughts grow in my head and need to find a way out—writing is my outlet. I can write them, look at them, deal with them, and sometimes even learn about myself. (Most writers I know are surprised by how much they learn about themselves through the writing process.) It's very important to me—so important, in fact, that my big discovery as a writer wasn't that I could write, but that I couldn't not write. It's just part of who I am, and I'm lucky to have discovered that.

I also enjoy the process itself. I love balancing the creativity with the rules. When you're thinking about story, character, and tone, it's pure creation, pure freedom. But you're also dealing with language, so there are strict rules. It's like a tango—you need your own passion, flair, and style, but the dance has certain steps, rhythm, and tempo you must follow. So when you actually sit down to write, something happens that's both planned and spontaneous. I'll sit down to write a story and I'll have tons of notes, outlines, and all that, but I really won't know until I write it how it's going to turn out. That's exciting.

Finally, I like getting my views "out there" for others to see. Some people tell me that my writing helps them see things differently, and to appreciate things more. Everyone has a gift, and I think once we find that gift, we're obligated—and privileged—to use it to make some contribution to our community. I try to do that with my writing.

Q

WHAT MADE YOU WANT TO BE A WRITER?

A

Well, funny thing—I didn't!

And that's one reason I know I really am a writer. I never set out to be one, and I never really wanted to be one. But at some point in my life I discovered that I am one. That's how you know it's real. Of course at that point I started taking lots of writing classes and doing things that writers do, but that was all after the fact. The big moment was the discovery, and that probably came when my daughters were little, because I started writing about them—just describing them as little children—and before I knew it I had written an entire book about them. I didn't have a choice; I just did it, and I loved it, and I can't imagine not having done it.

When I started telling my friends that I'd made this discovery, and that I was a writer, they all laughed and told me they'd known it for years.

WHAT ADVICE WOULD YOU GIVE A FELLOW WRITER WHO WAS JUST STARTING OUT?

I had a terrific writing teacher once who told me: "I can't teach you how to write. No one can. That's because it's not something one person gives to another person. It's something you already have inside you. But what I can do is try to help you bring some of it out."

In other words, don't look to someone else to show you how to be a writer. You have an incredible, untapped talent inside you that is a million times more powerful than any teacher who ever walked the earth. Listen to that talent. Respect it. Find ways to bring it out! Your ways will be unique to you. Some people get up at 5:30 every morning and write ten pages. Some people write a poem on the bus. Some people dictate stories into a tape recorder. Some people jot down ideas for a year, and then type an entire best-selling novel in two weeks.

Follow your instincts. I've done a lot of writing and talked with a lot of people and you know what? The smartest person in the world can't write your story—the only person who can do that is you. They say you should ignore ninety percent of what your readers tell you, and I think that's true.

Do what you have to do. I went through a period of about five years when I couldn't read anything. I was writing all the time and couldn't bear to read even a paragraph of anyone else's work. Then I went through a period where I had to read all the classics—I devoured them, one after another. So do what feels right for you. Take classes, read Faulkner, attend workshops, join writers' groups. Or not.

Finally, remember that everyone out there thinks he or she is a writer, and a better one than you. They're wrong! Writing is an "invisible" talent. Opera singers and tightrope walkers can instantly prove their credentials to anyone, so nobody questions their ability. But writing is subjective, so prepare to be critiqued, panned, dismissed, and most of all, rejected. All great writers go through this, and you can too! It actually shows that you're doing your job. Go read those stories about all the publishers who rejected *Gone With the Wind* or more recently, the publishers who rejected the Harry Potter books. Can you imagine?

The day I stopped listening to critiques was the day I got rejection letters from two different publishers. One said they loved my book but they wouldn't publish it because the market for this kind of writing was too small. The other said they loved it but they wouldn't publish it because the market was too big! I laughed out loud.

Remember that writing isn't about you and the critics. It's about you and the page.

MEANINGFUL MEMORABLE MOMENTS

Words are amazing things. At least they are to me. I've always been fascinated by them—how they look, how they sound, what they mean. I guess this is a good quality for a writer. But it was something I felt even before I started writing. I think most people are captivated by words in some way, whether they think of themselves as writers or not.

Big words rarely fail to get our attention. When I was little, every kid on my block wanted to know how to spell "antidisestablishmentarianism." I never knew why exactly. I think someone said it was the longest word in the dictionary. None of us even knew what it meant, but that didn't matter. It was the length of the word—and its obscurity, I suppose—that fascinated us.

Years later, even when I discovered that it wasn't the longest word in the dictionary ("floccinaucinihilipilification" is one letter longer); even when I realized that spelling it was easy because it was just a bunch of normal words, suffixes, and prefixes jammed together (anti + dis + establish + ment + arian + ism); even when I finally looked it up and found that all it meant was wanting the Church of England to remain the official church of that country (I mean, seriously, how many kids in America care about that?); even after admitting that I have never in my life had occasion to write it or read it (except when I looked it up); even after all that, I still remember it, and it is, in some strange way, still one of my favorite words.

As I got older, I became more interested in small words. Bumping up against the challenges of adult life, words like "love," "hope," "faith," and "peace" began to command my interest. I guess when you're trying to find a job, a date, or a decent place to live, you don't care anymore what the longest word in the dictionary is, or whether you can spell it.

But when I hit my mid-thirties and started taking my writing more seriously, I realized there was more to good word choice than merely choosing good words. Good words are wonderful all by themselves, but they don't reach their full potential until they're arranged in good groups. This is often when we experience language at its best, when a writer turns a phrase so artfully we can't help but pause to examine it, savoring the moment and the meaning we've discovered.

These meaningful moments are the stuff of great reading. And readers take great satisfaction when they encounter them. But sometimes they take even more than that. We write to communicate. And while we hope to reach our readers as they read our work, we also hope they take some of it with them when they're done. Our goal isn't just to have readers understand our words as they go by, we want them to remember our words long after the final page has come and gone.

WHAT MAKES SOME WORDS MORE MEMORABLE THAN OTHERS?

When it comes to language, the human brain is staggeringly powerful and strangely deficient. Almost instantaneously, people can snatch words from a mental lexicon with tens of thousands of entries. But almost no one can remember the last fifty words of a conversation. Our brains have an extraordinary capacity for storing and retrieving words in long-term memory. But our short-term memory for language stinks. And this is why writers have to work so hard to come up with words their readers will remember.

A typical novel is 60,000 to 100,000 words long. Magazine cover stories often run 2,000 to 3,000 words. And at 500 to 1,000 words, even an essay by the average high school writer is much longer than the average reader can easily memorize. So what do we have to do to get readers to remember our words?

- **Get them to notice.** With all the words readers have to deal with, it's unlikely they'll take note of the ones we write unless we give them something special to notice. This means we have to take risks to express our ideas in unusual ways. We don't have to resort to obscure words our readers have never heard of. But we may want to consider putting familiar words together in unfamiliar combinations.

- **Get them to think.** Remembering something is often determined by how much time we spend thinking about it. If a reader reads 240 words per minute, that's only a quarter-second per word. If we expect readers to remember some of the interesting words and phrases we come up with, we need to slow them down a bit by presenting them with language that will keep them thinking beyond the brief moments they spend decoding.

- **Get them to feel.** As we read, every word we decode enters into our short-term memory for language. But few words stick around for very long thereafter. If we want our readers' short-term memories to become long-term memories, we have to stir their emotions. The more we can evoke strong feelings in our readers, the more likely they will be to remember what we write.

If we want our readers to remember our words long after they've finished reading, we have to give them writing that is worth remembering. Readers read to get meaning from text. So the more meaningful our writing is to them, the more memorable it will be as well. Meaning is made in the mind of the reader. But the words we write spark the meaning-making process. So how we can use our choice of words to light the fire of our readers' imagination and create meaningful memorable moments?

LOOKING AT MEANINGFUL MEMORABLE MOMENTS

My friend, Ben Hippen, wrote a wonderful short story called *Eddie Takes Off*. It's about an unusual boy who doesn't fit in very well with the rest of the world. There are many things I like about this story but what I like best is how Ben created so many meaningful memorable moments with his words. This story is packed with vivid verbs, clever modifiers, evocative expressions, and many a satisfying turn of phrase. Here are ten of my favorite sentences.

1. Eddie had always been able to fly, but it wasn't until his fifth birthday party that he realized that it would turn out to be a *bit of a social problem.*

I told you Eddie was unusual. Apparently he has been able to fly since birth and his parents have never known exactly what to do about it. The phrase I love is "a bit of a social problem." What an understatement! Eddie's parents know their little boy is in for all kinds of problems once people in town discover his secret.

2. Until that embarrassing day on the Johnsons' lawn, Eddie's parents had treated his *airborne peculiarity* as something of a childish whim.

Again, notice the understatement here in the words "airborne peculiarity." "Childish whim" is nice, too, though not as unusual. Most children are whimsical. But it sure would be peculiar if one of them became airborne.

3. Eddie's mother thought that perhaps they should take their son to see a specialist, but his father *vetoed* the idea.

"Vetoed" is a great verb. The author could have said that Eddie's father didn't like the idea or that he disagreed with Eddie's mother. But "vetoed" is so much better because it makes it seem as though Eddie's father has the power of a president or a governor who can't be overruled.

4. His father shot him a *look so full of "No!"* that Eddie desisted at once and sulkily spent the rest of the day firmly seated on the carpet.

I've never in my life come across the expression "a look so full of 'No!'" and yet I know exactly what that look looks like. Don't you? Hasn't your mom or dad or a teacher ever looked at you that way? It's even worse than having them say it, isn't it? When a writer can introduce his readers to language they've never before encountered, and communicate his meaning with perfect accuracy, something rare and wonderful is happening on the page.

5.   Alex began hitting Eddie with a *chubby, half-closed fist.*

In this moment, Eddie finds himself in a fight with a neighbor boy. Both boys are five years old and there's no better way to describe how little kids fight than to say that one hit the other with a "chubby, half-closed fist."

6.   His pleading was *swallowed by his mother's mortified silence.*

Think about this one for a second. There's no way silence can swallow anything. Nor can silence be mortified. And yet, these words make perfect sense in the story. Eddie has just done something he shouldn't have and embarrassed his mother in public. She's the one who's mortified. But as he pleads with her to understand why he misbehaved, she remains silent.

7.   And so Eddie made a promise to himself with *the intensity of a child's confused pain.*

Little kids get upset all the time. But sometimes it's worse than that. They get frustrated, angry, and finally confused. Then they seem to collapse into deep sadness. The phrase "the intensity of a child's confused pain" is a wonderful way to describe this.

8.   He would slowly levitate off the mattress, raising his brown comforter from underneath, looking *like a loaf of bread rising in the oven.*

Sometimes, when writers want to describe something out of the ordinary, like a boy levitating in his bed, they compare the unusual scene to something their readers can more easily imagine. When they introduce the comparison with the words "like" or "as," this technique is called a *simile*. Here, the words "like a loaf of bread rising in the oven" give us a perfectly playful picture of what's happening.

TIP:

Another way to make your words more memorable is to use a technique called alliteration. Alliteration occurs when words that are close to each other in the same sentence begin with the same sound, like the words in the phrases "perfectly playful picture" or "meaningful memorable moments." We'll talk more about this technique in "Chapter 7: Better Sentences."

    9.   Eddie twitched with *a spasm of heartache.*

When we're very sad we feel like our hearts ache. But usually our sadness comes on gradually and we ache for quite a while. Here, Eddie experiences that feeling instantly, and his whole body reacts with a twitch.

    10.   He felt *the surprise in her arms* as they tightened around him.

This is another one of those impossible expressions that makes perfect sense in the story. How can someone have "surprise in her arms"? And yet, as the girl puts her arms around him, Eddie can sense that she's surprised by what she feels.

I don't know about you, but I'd be happy to have one of these moments in a piece of my writing. And this story has many. It's a wonderful example of effective word choice and a great piece to use as a model for your writing. If you'd like to read the whole thing, you can download it here: www.eddietakesoff.com.

THE SECRET SAUCE

I've always wished there was a technique I could learn that would help me write sentences like these. But in twenty-five years of studying writing, I haven't found one. However, there does seem to be a pattern. And by figuring out how that pattern unfolds, you can learn to reproduce it in your work.

Lines like these call attention to themselves because of their uniqueness. But they do more than that. They not only get our attention, they hold onto it, as we find ourselves hovering over them for a few extra moments, puzzling out their meaning. Why do these phrases have such a strong effect on us? Because in almost every case, they pair ideas together that aren't normally associated with each other in our minds. For example:

airborne	+	peculiarity
a look	+	so full of "No"
a chubby, half-closed	+	fist
swallowed	+	by his mother's mortified silence
a spasm	+	of heartache
surprise	+	in her arms

If the story says that Eddie did something wrong and his father "shot a look" at him, in my mind I'm thinking "angry look", "threatening look", or maybe "a look of disapproval". But I'd never in my wildest dreams expect to find a look "so full of 'No'". It's no surprise, then, that this unusual choice of words might get my attention. And if I know two kids are fighting, I expect their fists to be balled up tight and strong. I don't associate "chubby" and "half-closed" with someone who is making a fist to fight—even if that someone is five years old. But perhaps the most interesting phrase of all is this one: "swallowed by his mother's mortified silence". I think that what makes this phrase so special is that it has a second unusual pairing (mortified + silence) inside it. That really makes us take notice—and take longer to figure out what it means.

These unexpected word combinations are called *juxtapositions*. To juxtapose two things means to put them side-by-side to see how they contrast. When writers put two unusual words together, readers experience the pleasure of teasing out the differences between the meaning they expect and the meaning they infer.

THE TRUTH ABOUT CREATING MEANINGFUL MEMORABLE MOMENTS

The first time I noticed the way great writers create great language by putting unusual words and ideas together, I got very excited. Eureka! I thought to myself. I've discovered the secret. Now I'll be able to write like that, too. Unfortunately, it didn't work out that way. For a while, every time I sat down to write, I tried to force words to come together in unusual ways. But all I got was unusually bad writing.

This doesn't mean that the pattern we just learned about isn't useful, or that you can't apply it to your own work. It just means that you'll probably be more successful if you think less about being a "great writer" creating "great language" and focus instead on doing a great job of being yourself.

Keep in mind that finding the right words may be more about reading than it is about writing. Great writers create great language not because they write so well, but because they are alive to the wonderful ways words create meaning in the minds of their readers. To do this, they have to be great readers, too. So as you think about how to improve the words you use, think less about conjuring up great language when you write, and more about hunting down great language when you read.

Read Like a Writer:

Hunting Down Great Language

Try copying down your own set of ten favorite sentences from every good book you read. It takes only a little while to do, but the benefits stay with you forever. Keep a reading journal with you as you read, and jot down great bits of language as you run across them. Then, later on, type them up and annotate them by writing down a few sentences that explain why you think they're so good.

WORDS THAT WORK

Good word choice doesn't mean using big words, it means using just the right words. The piece below is a good example of this. With everyday words and phrases, young writer Bojia Chen tells an entertaining story about an epic battle with bees.

Yellow Horror

As I grabbed the shovel with both hands and gave the dirt a jab, a big clump of earth broke into pieces, and from the crack in the ground came a wisp of yellow smoke that soon turned into a mass of yellow fog. The fog was a foot away from my face when I realized it was a swarm of yellow jackets.

I dropped my shovel and ran. I saw my pool, should I jump in? Nah, the pool would be freezing, so I took a sharp right for my house. I didn't dare look back; I was sure the angry swarm was right behind me.

Then I saw it. Oh, I'm saved, I'm saved, I'm saved! Sweet salvation! There it was: a can of "Guaranteed Kill, Yellow Jacket and Hornet Killer" sitting on a platform under my deck where I had left it just the day before.

I was still afraid to look back, so I snatched the can and ripped off the cap. As a bee buzzed just inches from my face, I did a quick 180-degree turn and pulled the trigger. There were dozens of them everywhere.

Unfortunately, I found out that the can I was counting on wasn't to be trusted. It wasn't a spray but more like a jet of expanding foam. The jet made contact with only a few yellow jackets, but I still had a million more to worry about, and they were all very angry now. My only choice was to run for the house.

Little did I know that a yellow jacket had flown up my shorts. When I raised my leg to climb the back steps, my pants tightened around the little invader and he stung me. I felt an instant wave of dizziness and almost collapsed on the stairs.

After stumbling into the house, I told my mom about the sting. She applied some of that weird gooey stuff all moms seem to carry with them for just these occasions.

It took a few hours for the yellow jackets to clear up, so I used the time to examine the can that I had hoped would save my life but didn't. That's when I realized that it wasn't for killing the insects, it was for destroying their nests.

Four hours passed and the yellow jackets still hadn't left. Determined to even the score, I put on a thick coat, four layers of sweat pants, a mask, and heavy-duty gloves. Then I went back outside to deal with them.

I read the directions on the can very carefully this time. Then I proceeded to the nest where I emptied the entire contents down the hole and waited as the foam expanded and overflowed. Almost immediately, the buzzing settled down. My heart stopped racing. And I never saw a single yellow jacket again.

You won't find a lot of fancy words here. But you will find words that work—language that tells an interesting story in a way that sounds true to the writer who wrote it. That's what we look for when we look for better words.

CONFESSIONS OF A WORD NERD

There's a wonderful book in my library called *Choose the Right Word*. It was written by S. I. Hayakawa, a former member of the U.S. Senate. But it's not about making political speeches. It's a usage guide.

What, you may ask, is a usage guide? And why would anyone pay upwards of $20 to own one?

A usage guide is exactly what it says it is: a guide to the effective use of language. As to why I'd rather have one on my shelf than a $20 bill in my pocket, the only answer I can give you is that I'm a word nerd. After all, who but a word nerd would care about the difference between gobbledygook, gibberish, and claptrap?

As I've already mentioned, the English language is full of words that seem to mean the same thing but actually mean slightly different things. For example, gobbledygook, gibberish, and claptrap all refer to language that is meaningless or otherwise difficult to understand. But each of these words has a deeper meaning:

- "Gobbledygook" is often used to describe language that is more complicated than it needs to be: "The contract my lawyer drew up was full of the usual gobbledygook."

- "Gibberish" is often used to describe language that may be appropriately complex for the subject matter under discussion but too complicated for certain readers to understand: "Any explanation of Einstein's Theory of Relativity would seem like gibberish to a fourth grader."

- "Claptrap" is often used to describe language that seems fake, insincere, or otherwise worthless, as though the person using it is showing off merely to appeal to an audience's emotions: "The mayor's speech riled up the crowd, but experts agreed it was mostly claptrap."

Even if we think these small differences in meaning don't matter much, we can't claim that they don't exist. Nor can we assume our readers lack interest in the matter. Word nerds are everywhere, and you never know when one will descend upon some words of yours. (Be on the lookout for people who love crossword puzzles or who seem to become overly excited by the mention of a game of Scrabble).

Miss Margot says

Word nerds can be fun to hang out with, and can help you become a better writer. If you know some good crossword puzzlers, lean over their shoulders next time and ask them how they figure out all those strange clues. And if you have a chance to toss tiles with a championship Scrabble player, don't hesitate to fill up a rack and sit down at the board. You'll be amazed at all the new words you can learn.

Then there's your future to think about. How well you do in high school, college, or on the job may depend at times on the breadth of your vocabulary. And since the best way to learn new words is to use them, a little word nerdiness on your part may help you get ahead in life.

Finally, if we're going to be serious about becoming better writers, I think we owe the language that gives us our most basic ingredients a little respect. English didn't just pop up overnight. Like our parents and teachers, and even yours truly, English is old—really old. It out-lasted the Roman Empire and was present at the signing of the Magna Carta. It served in the Revolutionary War, the Civil War, and two World Wars. It prospered in the Great Depression and has survived earthquakes, floods, fires, and locusts. Regardless of how tedious, tortuous, and downright confounding it can be at times, it deserves to be honored by those of us who take such interest in its use that we deign to call ourselves writers.

LEVELS OF MEANING

When we say that gobbledygook, gibberish, and claptrap are synonyms, what we're really saying is that they share the same general meaning. But each has a specific meaning that is slightly different. Like the difference between a weak verb and a strong one, knowing the specific meaning of a word helps us make the best choice when we have a list of synonyms to choose from.

There's another interesting way words can differ from each other even when they share the same meaning. Take, for example, the words "house" and "home." If I said, "I'll be at my home tonight after work" or "I'll be at my house tonight after work," I'm pretty sure everyone would agree that I said the same thing in both sentences. After all, "house" and "home" are synonyms.

But when we think of what the two words mean on another level, we immediately notice important differences. A house is a particular kind of building (distinct from an apartment, for example) where people live. A home doesn't have to be a building at all. In fact, the word "home" causes us to think about many ideas that have nothing to do with buildings: the place where our family lives, the town we were born in, or even feelings of safety and security. These other meanings, or associations as they're sometimes called, come from other ways of using the word:

- "I feel at home here" = comfort
- "Home is where the heart is" = love
- "It's great to be back home again" = belonging
- "This feels just like home" = familiarity

Word nerds like me use the terms "denotation" and "connotation" to talk about these different levels of meaning. Denotation refers to the simplest and most common dictionary definition of a word, sometimes called its "literal" meaning. Connotation refers to the collection of related ideas or associations a word has accumulated from being used in different ways. This is sometimes called its "figurative" meaning. "House" and "home" share the same denotation: a dwelling where people live. But they have very different connotations. Just think about the differences between these two sentences:

1 During his time at Hogwarts, Harry Potter lived in the House of Gryffindor.

2. At the end of his first year at Hogwarts, Harry Potter returned home to live with the Dursleys on Privet Drive.

In Sentence #1, "house" refers not only to a physical structure but to a special kind of membership in a special kind of community. In Sentence #2, "home" refers to a place where someone grew up. Both words refer to dwellings, but no self-respecting Harry Potter fan would ever argue that Harry's house and Harry's home were anything alike.

FROM CONNOTATION TO CONTEXT

If synonyms with different meanings aren't frustrating enough for you, and technical terms like "denotation" and "connotation" haven't discouraged you from learning more about words, there's one last idea I'd like you to consider: A writer can understand both the general meaning of a word or phrase, all of its specific meanings and associations, even its complex connotations, and still not use it effectively in writing.

Take another look at this sentence: "The contract my lawyer drew up was full of the usual gobbledygook." Here, the verb "drew up" means "wrote," as in "The contract my lawyer wrote was full of the usual gobbledygook." Now, you could also write this: "The speech the mayor wrote was nothing but claptrap." That works, too. But this doesn't:

"The speech the mayor drew up was nothing but claptrap." You can draw up a contract, you can draw up a list, you can probably even draw up a plan. But you can't draw up a speech. It just isn't done.

In order to make "draw up" work this way in a sentence, we have to understand its denotation ("to compose or create"), its connotation ("a sketch, a picture, a diagram"), and the context in which it is being used ("a legal document representing an understanding between parties"). Context in this sense means how it interacts with other words in the same sentence. Certain words, like "draw up," are used in certain contexts, like legal agreements, but not in others, like speeches. And that's another reason why we can't substitute synonyms for each other any time we want.

Denotation, connotation, and context. That's a lot to keep track of. And yet, we all instinctively keep track of these complex language elements every day. We just don't think about stuff like this until someone points it out to us—either in a learning situation or, worse, when we've made a mistake and someone misunderstands our meaning.

Miss Margot says

One way to check yourself is to read your sentence out loud. Sometimes, we aren't even aware that we know the connotation or proper context of a certain word. But we know when we hear it that it isn't right, even if we don't know why. This is always a good first check.

THE MEANING OF IT ALL

By now you're probably thinking that this entire section on knowing the meanings of words is nothing but gobbledygook, gibberish, and claptrap. But in our never-ending quest to find the right words for our ideas, this is exactly the kind of information we need.

In school, we often study *what* words mean. But rarely do we think about *how* words mean. It's all well and good to memorize dictionary definitions, but since few of your readers are likely to have done this, you may be disappointed to discover that their interpretations differ from yours, even on words you both claim to know.

I wish I could tell you there was a book you could read that combined dictionary definitions, synonyms, connotations, usage guidelines, and examples of words and phrases in common contexts. But there isn't. At least not one book anyway. Even Senator Hayakawa's book doesn't get the job done. Your best bet, if you're really serious about your words, is to get a copy of the *Oxford English Dictionary*. But then, you'll have to get a room to put it in, too, because it's over 20,000 pages long! (Thankfully, it's now available on CD-ROM so you don't have to build an addition to your house to own it.)

BUILDING YOUR VOCABULARY

It would be hard to get through school without having to do a few vocabulary exercises. Most of these will probably involve memorizing the definitions of long lists of words. Work hard at this, and do your best. But don't count on this activity to help you much as a writer. Studying words one at a time outside of the natural contexts of reading, writing, speaking, and listening isn't as helpful as teachers and textbook publishers think it is.

What is helpful is studying words as they come up in real life. Here are three ideas about how to do that:

- **Pay attention to unusual words and phrases.** Yes, there's a lot to know about words and there are a lot of words to know about. But ninety-nine percent of what we hear and read is already in our vocabulary. It's that other one percent we need to focus on. It's natural, especially when we're reading a long novel, to skip over the few words we don't know. Rarely does the outcome of a conflict or the fate of a character hang on our understanding of a single word.

But stumbling upon an unusual word is the best opportunity we have to learn it. Even if you don't want to stop reading to look it up, take a few seconds to make an educated guess about what you think it might mean. You'll be surprised how many words you can learn with this informal approach.

- **Be curious about connotation and context.** While it's good to know the definition of a word, if you're a writer that's probably not good enough. Connotation and context are often more important. When you see or hear an interesting word, ask yourself questions like, "Why was that word used instead of another word that means more or less the same thing?" or "What are some other ways I've seen or heard that word used?" or "What word would I have chosen if I was the speaker or writer?"

- **Start using a variety of word resources.** Until I came across Senator Hayakawa's book, I had no idea there was such a thing as a usage guide. I never knew there were different kinds of dictionaries, either. For example, the *Oxford English Dictionary* is a historical dictionary. It not only has the current meanings of English words, it tells you how meanings have changed throughout the history of the language. There are also many valuable word resources on the Internet.

Some people would say that to be a writer you have to build a big vocabulary. But I wouldn't be one of them. In fact, I might argue that it's the other way around: You have to be a writer to build a big vocabulary.

We tend to learn best by doing things. And when we're doing something we care about like writing, we tend to learn a lot. Our quest to be better writers leads us naturally to better words. We start to take risks by using new words that interest us. But we check these words out using dictionaries and other resources. In time, adding words to our vocabulary is as normal as reading a book or picking up a pen.

ACTIVITY: COLLECTING WORDS AND PHRASES

At one time or another, most writers have kept a small collection of interesting words and phrases. It's time to start keeping yours. When you come across a tiny bit of language that you like, jot it down on a pad. You may also overhear interesting words and phrases on television or in everyday conversation. Think of the world around you as a dictionary and a usage guide. Turn your life into a vocabulary lesson.

Miss Margot says

There are two words I really like. Unfortunately, neither of them comes up regularly in my conversations or my writing. But I like them just the same. The first is "tocsin," which sounds like "toxin" but means something totally different. Rather than something hazardous or poisonous, a tocsin is an alarm bell or a warning signal. The other is "desideratum," something that is both desired and required. I don't know why I like these words, but I came upon them in my reading, made a note of them, and they've stuck with me ever since.

MATCHING WORDS WITH READERS

Yesterday there was a fight at school. You weren't in it but you saw the whole thing and people have been asking you about it ever since. After school, your best friend wanted to know what happened. Your mom got wind of it and asked you at the dinner table. The next morning, your teacher wanted to know about it, too. And finally, at lunch, the principal called you into his office. (Don't worry, you aren't in trouble; he just wanted to get the facts from someone who wasn't involved.)

You've now told the story four times to four different people. Each time you've told it, you've recounted the same events. But you've used different language. With your friend you were casual, you even used some slang. With your mom you were a little more formal but you didn't worry too much about what you said. When your teacher asked you about it the next morning, you felt differently, and you spoke a little differently, too. But when you got to the principal's office, you were suddenly choosing your words with extreme caution, taking care to be as accurate as possible, speaking in crisp complete sentences, even throwing in a few "Yes, sirs" and "No, sirs."

You're the same person you were the day before when the fight broke out. And you haven't lied during any of the four retellings. But you definitely used different language each time. Why? Because you know that the way you speak to your friend on the playground is not the way you speak to the principal in his office.

Some people would call this respect. Others might say it was just good communication skills. But no matter what you call it, we all know how to do it. Every one of us knows how to change our spoken language to meet the requirements of the different people we talk to and the different situations in which we find ourselves. But sometimes when we're writing, we mysteriously lose this natural ability.

We don't actually forget what we know about talking to people, we forget that we're talking to people at all. Sitting in the principal's office it's impossible to imagine that the large imposing former football coach who has the power to change your life in a nanosecond is not actually right there in front of you. But when you're writing at your computer at home, or working at your desk in class, it's easy to forget about your audience—and to forget about the kind of language you should be using to address them.

CASUAL CONVERSATIONS

When we speak to someone, we know exactly who's listening to us. But when we write, it's easy to believe that the only person reading our words is us. It's as though we're talking to ourselves. And when we talk to ourselves, we tend to talk casually. As a result, we write casually. And that's where we often get into trouble with our word choice.

If you're writing something for your closest friends, this probably won't be a problem. But if you think any of your readers will be adults, or other kids who don't know you, you may have to shift your language into a higher gear, and write more formally if you want to be taken seriously.

In terms of word choice, what does writing more formally mean? In general, it means using standard grammar and conventional spelling, and avoiding slang. It's not that the words you and your friends use in conversation are bad. But when you're communicating with people who are a lot older than you, people who live in a different place, or even other kids who don't know you very well, you may find that the words you use in your everyday life aren't easily understood. Even worse, if you aren't conscious of who you're writing to, you may offend someone.

 *Miss Margot says*

I'm from the South and we have certain ways of saying things. If you're not from the South, you might not even understand what I'm talking about. Most of the expressions I use are not offensive per se, but they sure can be hard to follow for folks who aren't from the same region.

THE CHOICE IS YOURS

You really do have choices when it comes to the language you use. Your vocabulary has thousands of words in it. And the English language you're drawing from has thousands more you will undoubtedly come to know. But when it comes to using language appropriately, it's the words your readers know, and the meanings they associate with them, that matter most.

Some people are deeply offended by certain words and phrases. You have no control over this, and no responsibility to change your beliefs as a result. But if you want to be an effective writer, one who can reach most people and influence them, you need to think about who your readers are and how they are likely to react to your use of language.

As we discovered in the previous section, we not only have to know what words mean to use them well, we also have to know what context to use them in. We defined this linguistic context as the way words worked together in the same sentence. But there's also a social context when we write that is defined by our relationship to our readers and the reason we are writing to them.

When I was little, my parents taught me certain rules about talking and behaving in different social situations. Like many kids, I thought these rules were stupid. I couldn't remember them all, and many of them seemed unnatural to me. It wasn't until I became an adult that I began to understand why it was important for me to learn these things. As a kid, I thought manners and politeness were just a way for adults to control me. But now I realize that these social graces, as they're sometimes called, aren't about me at all, they're about the people I socialize with. The purpose of being polite is to make others feel comfortable—even if I'm uncomfortable doing it.

The same thing goes for writing. You have many ways of using language that are normal and natural to you. But when you write to certain people for certain reasons, your normal, natural way of conversing may not be comfortable to the readers you're trying to reach.

From time to time, we all have to change the way we talk in order to get people to listen. This may not be fair, but it's certainly true. In my own writing, I'm often frustrated by this. I have things I want to say and people I want to say them to. But as soon as the words pop onto my computer screen, and I begin to read them back, I know there's no way in the world my words will work for my readers. So I sit on the backspace key for a while, and then I try to come up with something else. I guess I've decided that writing for my readers is more important than writing for myself. This is a choice you'll have to make almost every time you write.

CHAPTER SEVEN

Better Sentences

TEN THINGS YOU NEED TO KNOW
EVEN IF YOU DON'T READ THIS CHAPTER

1. To learn how to write great sentences, we shouldn't write the way we talk, we should write the way we read.

2. Starting sentences with the same words, over and over, can be incredibly annoying to readers. Whenever our ears pick up a repeating pattern, that's what we focus on.

3. A long sentence is a thing of beauty, and that's probably why so many writers love to write them. But readers like variety, with a mixture of long and short sentences.

4. Knowing how sentences are constructed is important. But it probably won't make you a better writer. Practicing sentence patterns, however, will.

5. A great way to improve your eye for great writing is to create a Sentence Hall of Fame that includes the best sentences you read and the best sentences you write.

6. Long sentences are great, but sentences that are easy to understand are better.

7. Sentence length is one of the most important aspects of readability.

8. Writing readable sentences is both a science and an art. While there are technical considerations to keep in mind, your ear should always be the final evaluator.

9. The best sentences, regardless of how long and complex they may be, are always easy to read with expression.

10. There are many techniques writers use to make their writing sound as interesting as it reads. Most are associated with poetry, but they work just as well in prose as long as you don't overuse them.

SERVING YOUR SENTENCE

Every writer serves a sentence: a lifetime of ideas imprisoned between a capital letter and a period. But it's not so bad in there. Got a verb to keep you company. Usually a subject, too. Not to mention direct and indirect objects, maybe even the occasional preposition. Sure, it gets hard sometimes. You feel like you want to break out—use a fragment, write a haiku. But you always come back to where you belong, the place where everyone understands you.

Forgive me if I wax poetic about the most important structure in the history of prose. It's just that sentences are so crucial to our work. And working to build better sentences is one of the best ways to become a better writer.

Sentences are also something most of us struggle with at one time or another. I've always had trouble understanding exactly what sentences are, how they work, and why mine are often more complicated than they need to be. I'd like to tell you that by following a few basic rules, you can learn to write perfect sentences every time. But it's not that simple.

In school, our teachers tell us things like, "Every sentence has a verb," or "Every sentence has a subject and a predicate." These things are mostly true, but they're also mostly useless. Writers don't write good sentences by keeping track of grammar rules.

So what do writers keep track of when they're writing good sentences? Here are five things:

- **Using a variety of different beginnings.** Readers get frustrated, and our writing becomes difficult to understand, when we start every sentence with the same words. Varying the way we begin sentences makes our writing more readable and more interesting. It also keeps our readers from tearing their hair out.

- **Using a variety of different lengths and structures.** Not only do we want to mix up our sentence beginnings, we want to mix up our sentence lengths and structures, too. Running too many short sentences together can be irritating; using too many long sentences in a row can cause our readers to feel fatigued.

- **Structuring sentences so they're easy to understand.** Sentences are made up of parts that can often be ordered in several different ways. But some orders are easier to understand than others. So we try to structure our sentences in ways that make our ideas as clear as possible.

- **Creating writing that is easy to read expressively and that sounds great when read out loud.** Sentences not only have to make sense, and fulfill certain grammatical obligations, they also have to read well, too. This is the part of writing words that is similar to writing music. To fully understand what we write, our readers have to read with expression. Expressive reading involves making changes in pitch, rhythm, volume, and timbre. Well-crafted sentences make expressive reading easy and enjoyable.

- **Using rhyme, alliteration, and other "sound" effects.** Even though we're not writing poetry, we can still use the sounds of words to create an interesting experience for our readers. Here again, variety is crucial. Like repetitive sentence beginnings, and too many sentences of the same length, sentences containing too many words with the same sound can make our writing hard to understand and drive our readers crazy.

People are fond of making comparisons between writing and speaking, but when it comes to writing better sentences, the comparison doesn't always hold up.

As a kid in school, I developed a great dislike for sentence-writing and grammar exercises. Even when I did them correctly, I felt like they were wrong somehow. I knew I was a pretty good talker. And even though I didn't like writing, I didn't have much trouble putting a few words down. But I hated grammar and sentence work; it just didn't make sense to me.

It wasn't until my thirties that I figured out what my problem was. I was trying to fit all those textbook rules to the way I spoke naturally. But, like most of us, my speech patterns were a little different from the grammar guidelines my teachers wished I would follow when I wrote.

I was missing a key piece of information: To learn how to write great sentences, we shouldn't write the way we talk, we should write the way we read.

Historically, the concept of the sentence wasn't created to help speakers, it was created to help readers. If I'm delivering my own address in the public square, I might not even need my words written down. And even if I do, how I choose to separate my ideas will depend more on the rhythm of my voice and the pace of my phrasing than it will on the locations of capital letters and periods on a page. After all, many speakers do just fine working from lists and notes that aren't even written in sentences.

Reading, not speaking, is the key to becoming a great sentence writer. Almost everything you read is filled with excellent examples of effective sentence construction. The best way to become a great sentence writer is to study the great sentences you read.

YOUR CHECKLIST FOR BETTER SENTENCES

Fixing your own sentences can be hard work. Things that sound good to your ears may not sound good to your readers' ears. Worse yet is the feeling you get when you're sure there's a mistake somewhere but you just can't find it. To make things a little easier, use this checklist when you review your writing:

You know you're writing great sentences when you:

Use a variety of different beginnings. Do you start different sentences with different words? Do you start different sentences with different parts of speech? Do you ever start three sentences in a row with the same words or parts of speech? (Watch out for these spots! They could be trouble.)

Use a variety of different lengths and structures. Do you mix long, short, and medium-length sentences throughout your writing? Are your sentences made up of different numbers of parts?

Structure your sentences so they're easy to understand. Have you arranged the information in your sentences so it's as easy as possible for your readers to understand? In long sentences, are you using connecting words and punctuation to string together sentence parts in ways that are helpful to your readers?

Create writing that is easy to read expressively and that sounds great when read out loud. How does your writing sound when you read it out loud? Is it easy to read with good expression? What are the most expressive parts?

Use rhyme, alliteration, and other "sound" effects. Where are you using rhyme, alliteration, and other "sound" effects? How do they make your sentences more interesting to read? Are you being careful not to overuse these techniques?

While each of these five elements is a necessary part of the care and feeding of healthy sentences, the true measure of sentence success is how your writing sounds when it's read out loud.

STARTING OUT RIGHT

Recently, I had a chance to work with a class of first graders. I started by helping them choose topics, of course, and the strategy I used was the Like-Hate T-Chart from Chapter 2. One little boy decided he was going to write about lunch. I could tell it was his favorite topic in the whole world because it was the only one he wrote down. All the other kids had five or six different topics on their lists. But apparently this little guy liked lunch so much that it crowded out every other possibility from his mind—or maybe he was just hungry.

Here's what Tyler wrote about lunch:

Lunch

I like lunch. I like grilled cheese sandwiches. I like fish sticks. I like milk. I like chocolate milk better than plain. I like dessert. I like lunch the best of all the things at school.

This is typical of the way many little kids write. Their pieces sound like lists, and they keep repeating themselves over and over: I like..., I like..., I like..., etc. I'm never sure if they mean to sound like this or if they just get the hang of writing the "I like" part and figure why bother using any other way to start their sentences. But even if they do like writing this way, I try to talk them out of it.

Starting sentences with the same words, over and over, can be incredibly annoying to readers. They just aren't used to taking in language like that. It sounds strange and, well, childish. It's also hard to understand. Whenever our ears pick up a repeating pattern, that's what we focus on. As soon as we start reading Tyler's piece, we get stuck on his "I likes" and forget what the piece is about. This can even happen to big kids like us, if we unknowingly use the same opening words to begin several sentences in a row.

To get Tyler to improve his sentence beginnings, I needed to have a conference with him. He was only six, so telling him to vary the beginnings of his sentences probably wasn't going to work. So I had him retell the piece to me rather than reread it. Immediately, his language became more natural. And so did the beginnings of his sentences. Eventually, he rewrote the entire thing from scratch:

Lunch

I like lunch. Grilled cheese sandwiches are good. So are fish sticks. Most of the time, I drink plain milk. But chocolate milk is better. Lunch is my favorite thing at school.

Not exactly Pulitzer Prize material, but it's a big improvement over the original. And the only thing he did, really, was change the way he started his sentences.

So here's a little rule of thumb: Don't use the same words to start a sentence three or more times in a row. Better yet, try to start every sentence a little differently if you can.

TIP:

Watch out for repetitive transitions. You might start repeating sentence beginnings somewhere in the middle of a piece and not even realize it, particularly if you're telling a story and you get stuck on using the same transition words over and over: Next..., Next..., Next..., or And then..., And then..., And then....

Take a look at my sentence beginnings from the opening section of this chapter:

> **Every writer serves** a sentence: a lifetime of ideas imprisoned between a capital letter and a period. **But it's not** so bad in there. **Got a verb** to keep you company. **Usually a subject**, too. **Not to mention** direct and indirect objects, maybe even the occasional preposition. **Sure, it gets** hard sometimes. **You feel like** you want to break out—use a fragment, write a haiku. **But you always** come back to where you belong, the place where everyone understands you.

Each sentence begins in a different way without even a hint of repetition. That's what you're looking for, too. And a great way to find it is to do exactly what I did here: Notice the first three words of each sentence, one sentence after another, and listen for repeats. If you find any, retell the sentence to yourself and fix them, just like Tyler did.

BE A WRITER LIKE DUNCAN MURRELL

Duncan Murrell is a writer and editor living in Pittsboro, North Carolina. He has worked at newspapers in Alabama, Washington, D.C., and North Carolina, in addition to writing for Harper's, Poets and Writers, The Oxford American, Mother Jones, Men's Fitness, *and other magazines. Duncan has covered science, crime, higher education, the arts, defense, intelligence, Congress, and the Pentagon. In 1997, the Associated Press named him the best young newspaper writer in North Carolina.*

Q WHAT KIND OF WRITER ARE YOU?

A I am a freelance magazine writer, a journalist, and a novelist. I'm currently working on articles, a novel, and a book of nonfiction.

Q WHY DO YOU WRITE?

A I came to writing because I was good at it, and because I had idolized authors growing up. They were rock stars to me. When my friends were turning me on to Hüsker Dü and The Replacements, I was handing out copies of *The Quiet American* and *Hell's Angels.* I thought the life of a writer would be filled with glamour. I began collecting typewriters.

After two decades of single-mindedly pursuing the life of a writer, I've made myself unqualified to do anything else, so you could say that the reason I write is because otherwise I'd starve. But that would discount the love I still have for it, and the powerful charge I get out of creation. I don't feel very well in the evening if I haven't written something that day. The life isn't glamorous, though, and most of the writers I know are nothing like rock stars. Most writers I know are shy, odd, and shockingly boring most of the time, at least outwardly—it's their inner life that roils and makes them write. The only thing you can hope to get out of writing is the writing itself, and maybe a little money. If it's fame and fun and guest spots on The Daily Show that you're after, you'd be smarter to become a politician.

Q WHAT MADE YOU WANT TO BE A WRITER?

A See above. Also, I like tweed.

Q WHAT ADVICE WOULD YOU GIVE TO A FELLOW WRITER WHO WAS JUST STARTING OUT?

A Educate yourself, either through formal education or through self-directed reading. In fact, whether you get a formal education or not, the lifelong pursuit of reading is essential. Write what you'd want to read, and never be ashamed of what that is. Send thank you notes and letters to people who help you along the way. Help other writers along the way. Finally, do what an agent friend of mine says he admires in the best writers: At some point in their lives, they stopped waiting for someone else to invest in their talent, and invested in it themselves. To him this meant taking a chance, risking failure and temporary financial ruin in order to do the best work he could possibly do. This friend of mine, who knows what he's talking about, says this is the mark of great writers. They have guts.

THE SPICE OF LIFE

They say variety is the spice of life. But it's also the spice that makes for a tasty batch of sentences. Not only do we need variety in the beginnings of our sentences, we need it in their lengths and structures, too.

Most sentences run between twelve and twenty words. The average length is probably around sixteen, though this can change a little depending on the kind of writing you're looking at. Fast-paced young adult novels might have slightly shorter sentences; formal scientific research papers might have slightly longer sentences.

For purposes of our discussion here, let's call a sentence of less than twelve words "short," a sentence of more than twenty words "long," and any sentence in between "medium." The basic idea in varying sentence lengths is the same as it is with varying sentence beginnings: Try to avoid having too many of the same kind in a row.

Here are the sentence lengths for the first four paragraphs of this chapter:

Paragraph 1: 17, 7, 7, 4, 12, 6, 15, 15
Paragraph 2: 16, 10, 17
Paragraph 3: 14, 29, 26, 21, 5
Paragraph 4: 22, 10, 11

That's a typical mix. Many of my sentences are right around the average length. But I've also got little clumps of short and long ones in there. (The really short ones aren't technically sentences; they're sentence fragments. A sentence fragment is a piece of a complete sentence—typically, the verb or subject has been left out—punctuated as if it were complete.)

Most writers don't have to worry about revising their short and medium sentences. It's the lohng ones that cause problems. Either we don't have any of them at all, or the ones we try to use get tangled up to the point where they don't make much sense.

ACTIVITY: HOW LONG ARE YOUR SENTENCES?

Find a finished piece of your own writing and count the words in a group of ten to fifteen sentences. What do you notice? Do you have a nice mix of short, medium, and long ones? Watch out for sentences that are really long—say, longer than forty words. You may actually have several sentences on your hands, and you just forgot to put in a period or two.

Miss Margot says

If you want to see some really long sentences, look at any story by William Faulkner or Charles Dickens. Man, could those guys string some looooooooooooooooooooong sets of words together! For short sentences done well, read some Ernest Hemingway. He writes powerfully using just a few words at a time.

LONGING FOR LONG SENTENCES

A long sentence is a thing of beauty, and that's probably why so many writers love to write them. Not all the time, mind you. But every now and then, a thirty- or forty-word stretch between capital and period feels great. As a writer, I've struggled for years to learn how to control long sentences. And as a teacher of writing, I've struggled to help students control them, too. The truth is, like Pinocchio's nose, the longer a sentence gets, the more trouble it seems to be in.

When you learn about sentence styling, it can be helpful to learn about sentence structure. Sentence structure is incredibly important. But it can also be incredibly hard to understand. Most of us don't think about the structure of our sentences when we speak and write; we construct them unconsciously. But if we want to improve our sentence structure, and especially if we want to learn from other writers as we read, we have to become conscious of how sentences are put together. Unfortunately, the traditional pedagogy of sentential analysis is fraught with arcane terminology, abstruse constructs, and preternatural techniques. In other words, it's about as easy to understand as that last sentence.

To make it easier for people to study sentence structure, I came up with a different way of describing sentences. This is not an "official" way. I've never seen it in a textbook or had it taught to me in a class. But I have found that it works for just about anyone—something that can't be said for the traditional sentence diagramming approach. (It's especially good for people like me who never understood traditional grammar in school and still don't!) So here's your introduction to Mr. Peha's Stunningly Simple Sentence Structure System.

Take a look at this smooth-sounding forty-one-word sentence:

> On a bitter cold winter morning, Malcolm Maxwell, a young man of simple means but good intentions, left the quiet country town in which he'd been raised and set off on the bold errand he'd been preparing for all his life.

Not bad, eh? And it wasn't very hard to put together. You'll notice that it's made up of several different parts. In our system, there are four kinds of sentence parts you can use:

- **Main Parts.** These parts usually contain the main action of the sentence: "Malcolm Maxwell,… left the quiet country town in which he'd been raised,…."

- **Intro Parts.** These parts often introduce other parts, especially main parts: "On a bitter cold winter morning,…."

- **In-Between Parts.** As the name implies, these parts go in between other parts. They feel like a slight interruption: "…a young man of simple means but good intentions,…."

- **Add-On Parts.** These are extra parts that convey additional information about any of the other parts: "…and set off on the bold errand he'd been preparing for all his life."

Using our system, we can describe the structure of the sentence like this: Intro + Main + In-Between + Main + Add-On. Here again are those five parts written out in order:

- **Intro Part.** "On a bitter cold winter morning,"

- **Main Part.** "Malcolm Maxwell,"

- **In-Between Part.** "a young man of simple means but good intentions,"

- **Main Part, continued.** "left the quiet country town in which he'd been raised,"

- **Add-On Part.** "and set off on the bold errand he'd been preparing for all his life."

And that's all there is to it. You can create new sentences by combining the different kinds of parts in different ways. To make longer sentences, just add more parts.

Read Like a Writer:

Learning the System

I certainly don't expect you to learn this system from one brief example. Fortunately, examples abound in your everyday reading. Take anything you're reading right now and look first for a two-part sentence. Name the parts in the order they occur. Do this a few times until it becomes easy for you, and then start looking for three-part sentences and four-part sentences. Some sentences may not be easy to classify. Don't worry about those for now. Look for ones that match the system and learn from those.

SENTENCE PATTERN PRACTICE

Knowing how sentences are constructed is important. But it won't make you a better writer. Practicing sentence patterns, however, will. But how do you practice sentences patterns? And how do you know which patterns to practice?

As I've mentioned all along, the great writers you read will always be your best teachers. In "Chapter 6: Better Words," we looked at ten examples from Ben Hippen's short story, *Eddie Takes Off*, to learn about effective techniques for better word choice. Here we'll look at ten more examples, this time focusing on effective sentence patterns.

I'll break each pattern down into parts, show you a model of that pattern from the story, and then give you an example sentence, based on the pattern, that I wrote for a story of my own. Think about my example, and then give it a try for yourself.

I've organized the patterns by order of difficulty, beginning with several you might already know. Practice them a little anyway. In fact, no matter how confident you feel in your sentence styling abilities, start with Pattern #1 and create three to five example sentences. Then move on to Pattern #2 and repeat the process with each succeeding pattern until you get to one that's too hard for you, or you master them all.

TWO-PART SENTENCES

It may seem silly to spend time practicing two-part sentences. Almost every writer does them naturally. But that's exactly why we need to practice them. The fact that two-part sentences come easily to us means that we probably don't pay much attention to how we write them. Conscious practice raises our awareness. It also helps us understand how these easy sentences serve as foundations for the more complicated patterns we're not quite as comfortable with.

Pattern #1: Intro + Main

Model: For the first week or so after the party, Eddie stuck to his promise.

Intro:	For the first week or so after the party,
Main:	Eddie stuck to his promise.

Example: As he walked slowly to the front of the class, Mr. Funston dreamed of Christmas vacation.

Pattern #2: Main + Add-On

Model: He felt embarrassed, ashamed that he had hurt his mother.

Main:	He felt embarrassed,
Add-On:	ashamed that he had hurt his mother.

Example: He stared at the blank faces of his students, perplexed that he had nothing whatsoever to teach them today.

THREE-PART SENTENCES

Three-part sentences are my personal favorites. In fact, looking over my own work in preparation for writing this chapter, I noticed that in some of my pieces, these are the most complicated sentences I write. Even if you never feel comfortable with four- and five-part sentences, I wouldn't worry about it. You could probably go your whole life as a successful writer by carefully mixing your ones, twos, and threes.

Pattern #3:   Main + In-Between + Main

Model: Jane, on the other hand, was all that Eddie could think about.

Main:	Jane,
In-Between:	on the other hand,
Main	was all that Eddie could think about.

Example: The Lesser Antilles, Funston realized, would be the perfect place for a warm winter hiatus.

Pattern #4:   Main + Add-On + Add-On

Model: He felt the first blow on his back, causing him to stumble and drop his bag, which was promptly kicked into the bushes by another of the three.

Main:	He felt the first blow on his back,
Add-On:	causing him to stumble and drop his bag,
Add-On	which was promptly kicked into the bushes by another of the three.

Example: Funston saw himself on the beach, baking in the mid-day sun, his trusty dog trotting to and from the hotel with tasty snacks and refreshing beverages.

Pattern #5: Intro + In-Between + Main

Model: And then, shortly before his fifth birthday, Eddie's mother received a phone call from her neighbor three houses down.

Intro:	And then,
In-Between:	shortly before his fifth birthday,
Main:	Eddie's mother received a phone call from her neighbor three houses down.

Example: Ten minutes later, having dismissed his students early to lunch, Funston sat at his computer hunting and pecking his way to a good deal on a two-week vacation to the West Indies.

Pattern #6: Main + In-Between + Add-On

Model: He slammed into Alex, who let Jane's wrist go, and crashed into the wall so hard that his head made a small indentation in the plaster.

Main:	He slammed into Alex,
In-Between:	who let Jane's wrist go,
Add-On:	and crashed into the wall so hard that his head made a small indentation in the plaster.

Example: Funston leaned back in his big teacher chair, forgetting about the twelve pounds he'd put on at Thanksgiving, and tumbled backward into the Halloween bulletin board he'd neglected to take down.

FOUR-PART SENTENCES

If four-part sentences seem a bit daunting, think of them as three-part sentences with one extra part. That's usually how they work anyway. And more often than not, the extra part is an add-on.

Pattern #7:   Intro + In-Between + Main + Add-On

Model: Finally, barely realizing what he was doing, he picked up the phone again, and dialed Jane's number.

Intro:	Finally,
In-Between:	barely realizing what he was doing,
Main:	he picked up the phone again,
Add-On:	and dialed Jane's number.

Example: Awaking in a daze, unable to recall his name or occupation, Funston staggered out of school, and headed for the airport.

Pattern #8:   Intro + Main + Add-On + Add-On

Model: For the young Eddie, flying was just another discovery about his developing body, like learning that he could reach out his arm and ring the bell on his cradle railing, or finding that he loved the taste of peas.

Intro:	For the young Eddie,
Main:	flying was just another discovery about his developing body,
Add-On:	like learning that he could reach out his arm and ring the bell on his cradle railing,
Add-On:	or finding that he loved the taste of peas.

Example: As strange as it may seem, Funston's trusty dog met him at the airport, carrying a large suitcase in his mouth, and struggling with a small beach umbrella in his curled tail.

FIVE-PART SENTENCES

Once you start practicing five-part sentences, you're up in the strato-
sphere of sentence styling. The air is thin up here, no doubt about
it, so if you feel a little dizzy, slow down, catch a breath, and move
forward one part at a time.

Pattern #9: Main + Add-On + Add-On + In-Between + Add-On

Model: He walked down the sidewalk, lost in depressing
thoughts about school, until he became aware,
seconds too late, of the footsteps of three boys
running up behind him.

Main:	He walked down the sidewalk,
Add-On	lost in depressing thoughts about school,
Add-On:	until he became aware,
In-Between:	seconds too late,
Add-On:	of the footsteps of three boys running up behind him.

Example: They dashed down the jetway, dreaming of warm
sand between their toes, until it became apparent,
as a determined stewardess moved toward them,
that dogs with beach umbrellas could not ride in
first class.

Pattern #10: Main + In-Between + Main + Add-On + Add-On

Model: Eddie and Alex, after some preliminary shyness, got down to the serious business of playing with a set of toy trucks, and eventually seven other youngsters arrived, escorted by various parents and babysitters.

Main:	Eddie and Alex,
In-Between:	after some preliminary shyness,
Main:	got down to the serious business of playing with a set of toy trucks,
Add-On:	and eventually seven other youngsters arrived,
Add-On:	escorted by various parents and babysitters.

Example: Funston and his trusty dog, tired and hungry from their morning romp on the beach, found a rock where they could eat their lunch, and began to unpack their sandwiches, encouraged by a flock of seagulls who invited themselves to the party.

ACTIVITY: SENTENCE HALL OF FAME

Every time you read, you come across different kinds of sentences. Most are nothing special. But occasionally you'll find one that truly stands out. Maybe it'll be a long one with a dozen different parts. Or maybe it'll be a set of short ones, clustered together with an interesting rhythm. No matter what, write it down somewhere. Create for yourself a Sentence Hall of Fame that includes the best sentences you read along with the best sentences you write. Analyze their constructions, using the system we've learned here, and then, once you've unlocked the pattern, practice it over and over.

Miss Margot says

I should probably practice my long sentences, too. In journalism, we're discouraged from writing them because they can be hard to read within a newspaper or magazine layout. Plus, I tend to lose my own way in them. But sometimes, when I'm writing fiction, poetic prose, or any genre where I have a lot of freedom, I find myself chugging along—leaving strings of words in the wake of my ideas—and before I realize it, whaddaya know, I've written a 46-word sentence. Like that one.

ARRANGING AND REARRANGING

As soon as you start working with sentences made up of different parts, you start to notice that those parts can be ordered in several different ways. Take a look at these sentences, for example:

1. One of the interesting properties of sentences in most languages is that you can often rearrange the parts without changing the meaning.

2. In most languages, one of the interesting properties of sentences is that you can often rearrange the parts without changing the meaning.

3. Without changing their meaning, sentences in most languages can often have their parts rearranged—an interesting property.

I've just said the same thing three times, three different ways. The only difference was the sentence structure. The first and second sentences have basic one- and two-part structures: Sentence 1: Main; Sentence 2: Intro + Main. But Sentence 3 is much more complicated: Intro + Main + In-Between + Main + Add-On. Which one do you think is easiest to understand?

WHY SOME SENTENCES ARE HARD TO UNDERSTAND

Having fun with sentences is all well and good. But we have to remember that our writing will only be well-received if people can read it comfortably. Long sentences are great, but sentences our readers can understand are better.

While there are no hard and fast rules that I'm aware of regarding sentence readability, the following guidelines may be helpful. In general, sentences are more difficult to understand when:

- **They have too many parts.** I start to have trouble with my sentences when they stretch to four or five parts. Two- and three-part sentences are easy. After that, I really have to pay attention and do a lot of rereading to make sure everything's in order.

- **They have too many in-between parts.** In-between parts are probably the coolest sounding parts. But they're also the most troublesome. Coming as they do, in between other parts, they tend to break up the flow of normal reading. Most readers are comfortable with one in-between part in a sentence. But more than one can easily throw them off. For example: "The lanky left-hander, just up from AA and thrilled to be one rung further up the ladder to the Show, went into the stretch (he had runners on the corners, one out, and was looking for a pick-off or a double-play ball to get him out of a tough inning), peeked over his right shoulder, looked back at home to check off with the catcher, a trusted veteran who'd been stuck in the minors for years, and whipped around to nail his man at third." Too many interruptions in the main action of a sentence make it hard to follow.

- **They have too many add-on parts.** Add-on parts are my favorite parts because, as their name implies, you can just keep adding them on, one after another, until you've said everything you want to say, until you've exhausted all the possibilities, until you've left nary a trace of doubt as to meaning or intention, and your readers have grown weary searching for the light at the end of the tunnel—the period that arrives too late to keep them from putting down your piece and moving on to something else. Can you even remember where my sentence started or what it was originally about? I can't either. And that's the problem with too many add-on parts.

- **The main part comes late in the sentence.** The main part in a sentence typically contains the main verb, or main action, along with the person or thing that initiates the action. This is the part readers pay attention to most. Normally, we're used to finding the main part of a sentence up near the front. But sometimes writers postpone the main part like this: "As summer approached, and the days became warmer and longer, and the pace of life around our town began to slow like it always did when spring planting was over, and all a farmer could do was keep the birds and the bugs away and pray on Sundays for a little rain (though if last year's drought was any indication of our town's godliness, you'd think we'd be praying seven days a week by now), I took advantage of the free time I had and taught myself to write." Moving the main part to the end of a long sentence is sometimes a great strategy. But, like having too many parts at the end of a sentence, too many parts at the beginning can also make the writer's ideas hard to understand.

Much as readers love to read long sentences, and much as writers get a kick out of writing them, we're all better off when we can understand each other. Sentence length is one of the most important aspects of readability. If you've seen books at school that are marked with a certain grade level, you may have wondered why one book says fourth grade and another says seventh. Odds are that the seventh grade book has slightly longer sentences in it.

Writing readable sentences is both a science and an art. While there are technical considerations to keep in mind, your ear should always be the final evaluator. After years of dealing with my own sentence structure problems, I've made up a simple rule for myself: If a sentence sounds weird to me, it'll probably sound weird to my readers. Even if it looks right, with all the parts in order, if it doesn't sound right, I'm inclined to tinker with it until it does. Sometimes I have to put my writing away for a while and come back to it with a fresh view. But I always trust my ears, and not my grammar rules, when I make the final decision.

ACTIVITY: SENTENCE WRITING AND REWRITING

This may seem like a boring activity, but it's really, really good for you. Take any medium or long sentence you write and rewrite it as many ways as you can without changing the meaning too much. Do exactly what I did at the beginning of this section when I wrote the same sentence three different ways. Then, when you're done, read them all out loud and compare them for readability. Ask yourself if the order of the parts makes a difference in how they sound and how easy your ideas are to understand.

THE SOUND OF MUSIC

The page is alive with the sound of music. And the human voice is the world's most magnificent instrument. No member of the orchestra can match its majesty; not even the finest conservatory-trained virtuoso can coax out of wood or metal or string the rich varieties of tone and subtleties of expression that most of us can produce with our normal speaking voices.

Writing is written to be read, of course. But because we read silently, we don't think much about how our writing sounds. This can be a problem when it doesn't sound good to our readers. Strange phrasing, odd rhythms, and words that seem like sour notes challenge our readers as they attempt to perform what we have placed on the page. If there are too many challenges, they stop reading.

As strange as all this seems, writing a sentence really is a lot like writing a line of music for an instrument to play. In this case, the player is the reader and the instrument is the human voice. To interpret what we've written for them, either aloud or silently, readers read with expression—subtle changes in their voices that follow the structure of our sentences and the meaning of our words.

When I was in school, most of us read out loud like little robots, droning on mindlessly, word after tedious word, with no expression whatsoever. I don't know which was more embarrassing: reading out loud myself or having to listen to everyone else. Somewhere in the back of my mind, I knew that expressive reading was what my teachers did when they read to us. But I didn't know how to do it myself because I didn't know the four things good readers do in order to read expressively:

1. **They change pitch.** Expressive readers make their voices go up and down. They go up at the beginning of a sentence and down at the end. They also go up and down to differentiate the words of a speaker (often high in pitch) from those of the narrator (usually lower).

2. **They change rhythm.** Expressive readers speed up and slow down when they read. They also take appropriate pauses—big ones at the end of a sentence, smaller ones after commas, and even smaller ones between phrases.

3. **They change volume.** Expressive readers say some words louder than others. In general, the more important a word is the louder it is spoken.

4. **They change tone.** Sometimes readers use a soft, warm voice; at other times their voice is cold and hard. They do this to communicate different feelings—soft and warm usually means nice, calm, or even sad; hard and cold often means scary, angry, or excited.

When it comes to structuring sentences, pitch is the most important expressive reading component. So let's take a look at how pitch level corresponds to meaning and the four types of sentence parts.

- **Main parts are usually read at a middle pitch level.** This pitch level cues readers to the fact that this is the main action in a sentence.

- **Intro parts are often read at a higher pitch level.** This is especially noticeable when they introduce main parts.

- **In-Between parts are usually read at a level lower than the parts they are in between.** When an in-between part interrupts a main part, you'll sometimes feel your voice go very low.

- **Add-On parts are usually read at a level lower than the part they follow.** If a sentence ends with several add-on parts in a row, each one can be read slightly lower than the one that precedes it.

Finally, as we near the end of a sentence, our voice drops down to its lowest point—and often slows down a bit, too—as we reach the period. Here's a diagram that shows you exactly how all this works:

HIGH	On a bitter cold winter morning	
	INTRO	
MEDIUM	Malcolm Maxwell	left the quiet country town in which he'd been raised
	MAIN	MAIN, cont'd
LOW	a young man of simple means but good intentions	and set out on the bold errand he'd been preparing for all his life.
	IN-BETWEEN	ADD-ON

If you have trouble hearing these differences in pitch, don't worry about it. They're very subtle and most of us aren't used to listening for them. You may have to read out loud, or listen to someone reading to you, before you start to get the hang of it. To make matters even more complicated, the same sentence can be read in different ways by different readers. What you see here is the typical way readers change the pitch of their voice when reading a sentence with all the different parts in it.

Miss Margot says

Think about the people who do the news on radio and TV. Did you know that much of what they do is reading? It's true. But even if they're reading from a script or using a teleprompter, it sounds like they're just talking. This is because the writers work very hard to write good sentences, and the readers read very expressively. Pay attention the next time you watch or listen to the news, and you'll see—uh, hear—what I mean.

We change pitch when we read to help ourselves distinguish between different sentence parts. Since the parts of the sentence correspond to the parts of the idea the writer is trying to convey, changing the pitch of our voice improves our understanding.

The best sentences, regardless of how long and complex they may be, are always easy to read with expression. That's the true test. And while some of us can read expressively using only the quiet voice inside our heads, most of us need to hear our writing read out loud before we know for sure that it works. As awkward as this can be, it really pays to read your writing to yourself—in full voice and with plenty of expression. Better yet, get someone else to read it to you.

ACTIVITY: MIRROR, MIRROR ON THE WALL

Who's the fairest writer of them all? You'll never know until you read your writing out loud. Does reading out loud to yourself feel dumb? Why not try reading to yourself in a mirror? One teacher I work with wanted her students to do a better job reading over their work. So she put up a mirror in a back corner of her room so her kids could go up and read to it any time they wanted. They used soft voices and promised not watch each other or listen in. It worked great for them. Maybe it'll work for you.

LISTEN UP

In certain situations, sequences of speech sounds sometimes surprise us. Depending on how we count them, the English language uses forty-three or forty-four different sounds, and we can't help noticing at times how writers string them together.

There are many techniques writers use to make their writing sound as interesting as it reads. Most are associated with poetry, but they work just as well in prose as long as you don't overuse them. Like the sounds of the English language, you already know these techniques because you hear them every day. But you may not know their names, so here they are:

- **Consonance.** If you take the twenty-six letters of the alphabet and you throw out "a", "e", "i", "o", and "u", you're left with the consonants. ("Y" is both a vowel and a consonant, depending on how it's used.) When several words in a short sequence have the same consonant sound, we call the effect "consonance." For example, "He popped the cap and poured the gooey glop onto the paper."

- **Assonance.** The complement of consonance is "assonance." This occurs when several words in a short sequence have the same vowel sound. (Don't ask me why it's not called "vowelanance." I don't make the rules.) For example, "Everyone wants school to be better. But no one has an antidote for the glacial pace of change in education." Not only is the phrase "glacial pace of change" a good description of the situation, the repetition of the long "a" sound will make it stick in the reader's mind.

- **Alliteration.** When a group of words in a short sequence shares the same initial sound, we call it "alliteration". This is my favorite technique; I use it all the time, especially in titles and headings. For example, "Troubled teens face serious challenges these days. But we also have many wonderful ways to help them." I love starting a sentence with alliteration. Nothing kicks off an idea with as much energy.

- **Rhyme.** You know this one, of course. We say something rhymes when words in a short sequence share both ending vowel and consonant sounds. We all know poems that rhyme, but rhyme shows up every once in a while in prose, too. For example, "He might have to fight his arch rival in the next round."

Used sparingly, these kinds of "sound" effects can make writing fun to read and improve the flow of your sentences. They also make certain phrases easier for your audience to remember. Just make sure you don't overdo it—like I did in the first sentence of this section—because sentences with too many similar sounding words can be hard to understand.

HAVE YOU GOT GOOD SENTENCE SENSE?

When a young writer shows an ability to handle sentences with ease, we say that she has good "sentence sense". That's because just learning the rules of sentence writing doesn't always get the job done. Our language is so complicated that sometimes we have to rely on a writerly "sixth sense" to sort it out.

The writer below has great sentence sense. Her writing flows smoothly from phrase to phrase, reads well, and invites expression. There's never a place where I catch myself having to go back and read a sentence over to follow what she's trying to say.

There's No Place Like Home

On a dark December night in 1776, as he led a barefoot brigade of ragged revolutionaries across the icy Delaware River, George Washington said, "Shift your fat behind, Harry. But slowly or you'll swamp the darn boat." He was talking to General Henry Knox (they called him "Ox" for short). There's a painting of George Washington where he's standing up in a boat scanning the riverbank for Redcoats. I always thought he just wanted a good view. But I guess the reason he was standing was because he didn't have a place to sit down.

Finding a seat in his own boat was hardly the worst of General Washington's problems. It was cold and wet and icy, and his men were tired and didn't have warm clothes to wear or even enough food to eat. The Revolutionary War was hard on everyone, but it was hard on Washington most of all because he wanted to be home with his family.

From 1759, until he was called to fight in 1775, Washington lived with his wife Martha and her two children. Washington loved his big farm in Mt. Vernon, Virginia, and although he was one of our country's most brilliant generals, he was really just a farmer at heart. In a letter he wrote to a friend in England, he said, "I can nowhere find such great satisfaction as in working on my plantation." He didn't even want to be president. He said he would feel like a criminal going to his death if he took office. But everyone wanted him to do it, so he felt it was his duty to accept.

Washington was our president for the next eight years, but during that time he just wanted to get back home. He would spend weekends there whenever he could, and he made sure he got reports on the condition of his farm. He also liked getting letters from his family.

Then, in March of 1797, Washington finally got to go home for good. There were no more wars to fight, and John Adams was going to be president. Washington had been a good president, but he was tired of it. Even his granddaughter noticed how happy he was to be home. In a letter to a friend, she wrote, "Grandpa is much pleased with being once more Farmer Washington."

I always used to think of George Washington as a soldier and a politician, and I guess I always will. But he was really just a farmer. He reminds me a little of Dorothy from *The Wizard of Oz*. All she wanted was to get back home. And finally, the Wizard told her she could just click her red shoes three times and say, "There's no place like home." But George Washington and his men didn't have shoes when they crossed the Delaware River. Maybe if they did, history would have turned out completely different.

Not bad for a research report, eh? What I like best about this piece is that the writer brings all the creative energy and excitement of fiction writing into the often less interesting genre of research writing. This writer obviously knows how to find the story in history.

CHAPTER EIGHT

Better Punctuation

TEN THINGS YOU NEED TO KNOW
EVEN IF YOU DON'T READ THIS CHAPTER

1. If punctuation is a problem for you, welcome to the club. Most of us, including yours truly, struggle with it, too.

2. Instead of using a reference book to learn how to punctuate, you'll be better off using real books—and your own brain.

3. Don't follow rules mindlessly. As Pulitzer Prize-winning writer Donald Murray suggests, we're better off when we "...follow language toward meaning, always seeking to understand what is appearing on the page...."

4. To figure out if something is punctuated effectively, ask yourself four questions: How does it look? How does it feel? How does it sound? How does it mean?

5. When your writing changes, your punctuation may have to change with it. So if you learn to punctuate one way at one time in your life, you may have to make adjustments down the road.

6. To punctuate well, it helps to read well. Specifically, it helps to read with expression, even when you're reading silently.

7. To double-check your punctuation, read your writing out loud or have someone else read it to you.

8. One thing that makes learning punctuation hard is that different publications apply the rules slightly differently.

9. In general, writers use less punctuation nowadays than they did a generation or two ago. This is especially true of commas.

10. The best way to get better at punctuation is to ask more experienced people to help you figure out which marks you're using well and which ones you need to use more effectively.

DO RULES RULE?

Many people have problems with punctuation. Regular people have problems because they feel that they never learned the rules well in school. Writers have problems because they feel the rules don't always apply to them. Editors have problems (even though they know the rules) because the publishers they work for have additional rules of their own. And publishers have problems because they can't get the regular people, the writers, and the editors to follow their rules consistently.

So if punctuation is a problem for you, relax—you're in great company.

Because punctuation is so problematic, and even people who know the rules have problems applying them, I think it makes more sense to talk about how punctuation works in real books rather than in rule books. In fact, I think rule books might be why so many of us have so many problems with punctuation in the first place.

Miss Margot says

Because I majored in journalism, I have an entire shelf of rule books. Guess how many of them I use? None. Well, one, maybe twice a year.

THINKING RULES

So how are we going to punctuate our writing if we don't follow rules? We're going to take the advice of Pulitzer Prize-winning writer and writing coach, Donald Murray:

> The writer should not follow rules, but follow language toward meaning, always seeking to understand what is appearing on the page, to see it clearly, to evaluate it clearly, for clear thinking will produce clear writing.

Rather than memorizing rules, and then relying on them to tell us whether our writing is right, we're going to rely on our brains and evaluate our writing for ourselves. We're going to read our writing carefully, ask ourselves what we think it means, and think clearly about whether or not it will mean the same thing to our readers.

Any time you want, you can put this chapter down and grab a rule book. There's certainly no shortage of them, that's for sure. I think I have twelve. And I do look at them when I'm curious about something. But I don't use them when I write. When I write, I take Mr. Murray's advice, and instead of following rules I follow language toward meaning.

I also follow Mr. Murray's advice when I teach writing. That's why I'm more inclined to rely on real books than rule books when I want students to learn something new. As we read in class, we look closely at how writers and publishers punctuate their work. And when we see something that confuses us, we don't ask, "What is the rule?", we ask "What does it mean?" By looking at all the different ways punctuation is used, we develop the rules ourselves. Occasionally, when we're curious about something in particular, we use a rule book to look it up. But we always come back to real books—and real writing—to complete our understanding of how rules are applied.

Reading is all about getting meaning from text. But meaning isn't created on the page, it's created in the minds of our readers. And because the rules of writing aren't always in our readers' minds, we can't count on rules to help us communicate effectively. Readers will be using their brains to figure out what we're trying to say. So we're better off using our brains to say it as well as we can.

Let me be clear: rule books are useful references. Every writer should own several and consult them when they have specific questions. But rule books are hard to learn from because their rules are numerous and often difficult to understand. So why not supplement our rule books with the real books we read every day? We might discover unusual things from time to time, even things that break the rules. But we'll also discover what writing really is—communication between a writer sharing ideas through language and a reader following language toward meaning.

MEANING RULES

Since most of us are trained in school to follow the rules approach to punctuation, we might not know how to go about it any other way. What's all this "clear thinking" we're supposed to do? And what could be clearer than a rule?

Take a look at this sentence from *Eddie Takes Off:*

> He felt the first blow on his back causing him to stumble and drop his bag which was promptly kicked into the bushes by another of the three.

Now compare that one with this one:

> He felt the first blow on his back, causing him to stumble and drop his bag, which was promptly kicked into the bushes by another of the three.

Notice the difference? The top one has no commas, the bottom one has two. Which one is correct? What's the rule about commas? Hold on a second, I'll get one of my twelve rule books. Heck, maybe I'll get 'em all!

And that's the problem: When we punctuate by rule, we stop following language toward meaning and we start following a rule book—or twelve.

So instead of asking questions like "Which one is correct?" or "What's the rule about commas?" let's try questions like these:

- **How does it look?** At first glance, both sentences look fine to me. What I notice as I look more closely, however, is that in the version with the commas it's easier to see the three-part structure of the sentence. Without the commas, I can't tell until reading through it what the structure is. So I'm thinking that a reader might find the commas helpful if he or she is not used to reading sentences that are so long.

- **How does it sound?** Both sentences sound good to my ear. But when I read the first one, I find that I move along just a bit faster. That makes sense because the commas in the second sentence cue me to slow down just a bit at the end of each part.

- **How does it feel?** The first sentence feels slightly better to me. Without the commas, it reads like a single uninterrupted event. I also notice that it's a surprise action sequence. Apparently, our hero, the hapless Eddie, has suffered a sneak attack at the hands of evil Alex and his high school henchmen. It happens fast and I think that's why I want it to feel fast as I read it. The second sentence with the commas moves too slowly for me. It feels like three distinct slower actions instead one faster action.

- **How does it mean?** (Normally, we say "What does it mean?" but here we want to know how the punctuation affects what the sentence means and how the meaning of the sentence is conveyed to the reader as a result.) Neither approach to punctuation changes the meaning in my opinion. But there's a subtle difference in emphasis. Using the two commas to separate the three parts makes me feel as though they are of equal importance. Because of this, I tend to focus more on the last part where Eddie's bag goes under the bushes. In the sentence without commas, I pay a little more attention to the front of the sentence and come away with a memory of Eddie being pushed from behind. In either case, the difference is so subtle it's probably not worth worrying about.

So which way would I choose? I'd choose the no-comma approach for the reason I gave about wanting the speed of the sentence to match the speed of the action. However, at twenty-eight words, this is a fairly long stretch of language. If my readers weren't used to reading sentences this long, they might have some trouble. I'm thinking of kids as young as maybe third grade. You won't find a lot of twenty-eight-word sentences in third grade books. And if you do, they'll probably have commas in them. So if I'm writing for young readers, or for anyone who might lose their way in a long sentence, I'll take the two-comma approach.

Not surprisingly, my editor feels differently about this than I do. Here's what she has to say: "While the first sentence in your example is technically correct, most writers would choose the second sentence, simply because you can read it more easily and follow the action more clearly without getting mixed up. Most editors would say the two commas are necessary, because the second phrase is dependent on (or describes) the first clause, and the third phrase is dependent on (or describes) the second phrase."

Though I haven't looked it up, I'll bet my editor is right about the rules governing the use of commas in sentences with dependent phrases. And if you understand the concept of dependency in grammar, you may like that explanation, too. But I'm not sure she's right about most writers preferring the sentence with the two commas. In the first case, we can look in a rule book. In the second, we'd have to ask a lot of writers to know for sure. I asked five of my writer friends. Three liked the no-comma sentence, one liked the two-comma sentence, and one said that issues like this are just silly and that they don't matter to him at all.

One thing's for sure: When it comes to questions of punctuation, it seems like everyone has an answer—and that everyone is certain their answer is correct. Personally, I think it's great to have differences of opinion like these as long as everyone agrees that these are opinions, and that opinions don't become facts just because people repeat them over and over in a loud voice and bang their fist on the table. There aren't always clear right and wrong answers in the world of punctuation, especially when commas are involved. Some people think we have to play by the rules; others think rules were made to be broken. As for me, I think we all learn more, and get along better, when we follow language toward meaning, and leave the rules to the folks who write the rule books.

WHEW! THIS IS EXHAUSTING!

That was a lot of thinking for a couple of commas. If it's like that for every sentence we write, maybe a rule book's not a bad idea. But it's not like that for every sentence we write. In this particular case, we just solved a huge problem, one that is going to come up again and again for the rest of our writing lives.

The problem was this: Should we use two commas to separate the parts of a three-part sentence? And now we have our answer: If we want the sentence to feel like it's a single uninterrupted action, leave the commas out. If we want to slow our readers down, emphasize the three parts individually, or if we feel our readers might get lost along the way, use the two commas.

This won't cover every three-part sentence; some will require commas for other reasons. But it's a useful bit of knowledge that we'll be able to apply in many future writing situations.

Rather than following the words in a rule book, we followed the words on the page. We asked four important questions, and in the process, we learned something about commas—and about reading and readers and pacing within a sentence, as well as the relationship of punctuation to meaning, and probably several other things—that we can use for the rest of our lives. We can use our four questions for the rest of our lives, too. That's another reason why this way of doing things is probably easier than the rule book way. I know I can't remember a thousand rules. But it's easy to remember four questions.

So, yes, at any given moment, the "follow language toward meaning" approach to punctuation is harder than using a rule book. But if you're planning to write for the rest of your life, it's probably more efficient in the long run.

Miss Margot says

Most of the people I write for are more concerned with whether the meaning is clear than whether the punctuation is "right". To them (and to me, too) when the meaning's clear, the punctuation is right.

ORGANIZING OUR STUDY

In addition to setting aside the rule book, we might as well set aside the traditional notion of studying punctuation marks one at a time. The problem, for example, in studying a chapter on commas from your English book is that commas don't exist by themselves. They're also closely related to dashes and parentheses. Learning about commas in isolation won't prepare us very well for real-world writing. But if we study them along with the other marks of punctuation that are used inside sentences to separate the parts of an idea, we'll get a truer picture of how they work, and that will make them easier to understand.

For our purposes in this chapter, I'd like to focus on the five most important punctuation groups:

- **End-of-sentence punctuation that shows where ideas start and stop.** The capital letter that begins every sentence. The period, question mark, or exclamation mark at the end. And one unusual end mark that you've probably never heard of.

- **Middle-of-sentence punctuation that shows where parts of ideas start and stop.** The comma, of course, along with the other marks that help break sentences into parts: the dash, parentheses, the colon, the semicolon, and the mark that everyone loves to use—and overuse—the ellipsis.

- **Capitalization that indicates important words.** The basic rule is easy to remember but hard to apply: Capitalize names, places, and things that are one of a kind. But there are so many one-of-a-kind things that it's impossible to keep track of them. We'll see what we can do to sort this out.

- **Paragraphs that group related ideas together.** Like capitalization, the rules of paragraphing are simple. But figuring out how to paragraph is not. Grouping sentences together into paragraphs requires careful reading. And we can learn a lot by studying the way other writers paragraph their writing.

- **Dialog punctuation that indicates who is speaking and what is being said.** This involves several different marks: quotation marks, commas, and all the end-of-sentence marks. Also, everything has to be coordinated in just the right way. Punctuating dialog is probably the most complicated punctuation we can attempt.

Obviously, it takes time and effort to learn how to punctuate effectively. You may even have to learn things more than once. As you grow in your writing, your writing will change. And when your writing changes, your punctuation may have to change with it. That means that if you learn to punctuate one way at one time in your life, you may have to learn to punctuate slightly differently down the road. Learning to use punctuation effectively requires an on-going effort, one that develops over time as your writing develops.

This is another reason why focusing on meaning rather than on rules is a better way to learn. Every time your writing changes, the rules seem harder to follow. But to the writer who follows language toward meaning, the rules are always the same: read your writing closely, ask the four questions, analyze the work of other writers, and make decisions based on how you want your writing to be understood by your readers.

YOUR CHECKLIST FOR BETTER PUNCTUATION

To fix your own punctuation, you almost have to pretend that the writing belongs to someone else. And the best way to do that is to let your writing sit for a while—even a few days—before you try to edit it.

Effective punctuation involves using:

End-of-sentence punctuation that shows where ideas start and stop. Have you used capital letters and periods to show where your ideas begin and end? Have you remembered to put question marks at the ends of questions? Have you used exclamation marks sparingly, for excited utterances, only when you absolutely need them, and never more than one at a time?

Middle-of-sentence punctuation that shows where parts of ideas start and stop. Do you use commas to show where parts of sentences begin and end? Do you use dashes to emphasize in-between and add-on parts? Do you use parentheses to de-empha-size in-between and add-on parts? Do you use colons like an equals sign to show that one part of a sentence is an introduction to or description of another part? Do you use ellipses to show that part of a sentence is missing?

Capitalization that indicates important words. Have you capital-ized the names of people, places, and things that are one-of-a-kind? Have you capitalized the word "I"? Have you capitalized the first word of each sentence? Have you capitalized first, last, and important words in titles?

Paragraphs that group related ideas together. Is your piece written in paragraphs? Have you used paragraphs to group related ideas? Have you remembered to indent if you're using traditional indented paragraphing, or to skip a line if you're using block para-graphing?

Dialog punctuation that indicates who is speaking and what is being said. Have you put quotation marks around only those words that are actually spoken? Have you put ending punctuation that goes with quoted words inside the final quotation marks? Have you started a new paragraph for each new speaker?

Yes, there are a lot of questions here. But I don't expect you to be able to answer all of them at once. Concentrate on one group at a time. Start at the top with end-of-sentence punctuation and get that down first. Then move on. Don't feel that you have to learn all of this immediately. You've got plenty of time over the rest of your writing life to become a proficient punctuator.

PUNCTUATION READING

Why is punctuation so hard to learn? Because it's complicated and controversial, and the way we teach it in school often makes it confusing as well. We tend to make three mistakes when introduce kids to punctuation: (1) we focus on rules rather than on meaning; (2) we teach the marks in isolation rather than in the context of how writers use them; and (3) we teach punctuation with textbooks instead of with the real books we read every day. We've already dealt with the first two problems. Now we're going to tackle the third.

You probably remember this paragraph from the previous chapter. Give it a quick read once again:

> On a dark December night in 1776, as he led a barefoot brigade of ragged revolutionaries across the icy Delaware River, George Washington said, "Shift your fat behind, Harry. But slowly or you'll swamp the darn boat." He was talking to General Henry Knox (they called him "Ox" for short). There's a painting of George Washington where he's standing up in a boat scanning the riverbank for Redcoats. I always thought he just wanted a good view. But I guess the reason he was standing was because he didn't have a place to sit down.

Now read this:

> [NEW PARAGRAPH] [CAPITAL] on a dark [CAPITAL] december night in 1776 [COMMA] as he led a barefoot brigade of ragged revolutionaries across the icy [CAPITAL] delaware [CAPITAL] river [COMMA] [CAPITAL] george [CAPITAL] washington said [COMMA] [QUOTE] [CAPITAL] shift your fat behind [COMMA] [CAPITAL] har [HYPHEN] ry [PERIOD] [CAPITAL] but slowly or you [APOSTROPHE]

ll swamp the darn boat [PERIOD] [QUOTE] [CAPITAL] he was talk
[HYPHEN] ing to [CAPITAL] general [CAPITAL] henry [CAPITAL] knox
[PARENTHESIS] they called him [QUOTE] [CAPITAL] ox [QUOTE] for short
[PARENTHESIS] [PERIOD] [CAPITAL] there [APOSTROPHE] s a painting
of [CAPITAL] george [CAPITAL] washington where he [APOSTROPHE]
s stand [HYPHEN] ing up in a boat scanning the riverbank for
[CAPITAL] redcoats [PERIOD] [CAPITAL] i al [HYPHEN] ways thought he
just wanted a good view [PERIOD] [CAPITAL] but [CAPITAL] i guess the
reason he was standing was because he didn [APOSTROPHE] t have
a place to sit down [PERIOD] [END OF PARAGRAPH]

Pretty weird, huh? But it's also pretty interesting, if you ask me. This is
what reading is really like. Even though we don't say the punctuation
marks out loud, or even quietly in our heads, we do read over these
things every time we read. But we don't pay much attention to them,
and that's where we miss some valuable learning.

For example, in that single ninety-five-word paragraph, we encountered:

- **Forty-eight marks of punctuation.** And that doesn't include other
  conventions like the correct spellings of ninety-five words and the
  correct use of ninety-four spaces.

- **Ten different kinds of punctuation marks.** New paragraph,
  indent, capital, comma, quote, hyphen, period, apostrophe, paren-
  thesis, and end of paragraph.

- **Fifteen uses of punctuation.** Indent for new paragraph. Period at
  the end of a sentence. Capital at the beginning of sentence. Capital
  for a name. Capital for something that is one-of-a-kind. Capital
  for the word "I". Capital for a personal title. Capital for the name
  of a month. Parentheses for an aside. Quotation marks for dialog.
  Quotation marks for a nickname. Comma to separate parts of a
  sentence. Comma to introduce a quotation. Apostrophe for a con-
  traction. Hyphen to break a word at a line ending.

Is punctuation reading a good way to read? Hardly. It's very slow, and it's difficult to understand what you're reading. But it's a great way to learn about punctuation. It helps you learn the names of all the marks, and it helps you see how real writers use them in real writing.

PUNCTUATION READING: A LITTLE PRACTICE GOES A LONG WAY

When I teach punctuation reading in school, we try to practice it several days a week. But we only practice for a few minutes each day. Often we just read a single paragraph like we did in this chapter. For a couple of weeks, we concentrate on catching all the marks as we read. But we don't spend much energy thinking about why they're there. Then, when we get so good at reading punctuation that we can do it without thinking too much, we start trying to figure out how writers use it. So the next time you sit down with a book, spend the first two or three minutes doing a little punctuation reading. You might be surprised at what you notice.

Miss Margot says

I'm used to reading my writing out loud, but I'd never include the punctuation. When Mr. Peha first asked me to do it, I felt dumb. Then I started laughing. Now I think it's fun. I bet you will, too.

PUNCTUATION INQUIRY

Punctuation reading helps us learn the names of the marks and develop a sense for where they're used. But it doesn't tell us why they're used. For that, we have go to the next exercise: punctuation inquiry. Don't worry, it isn't as serious as it sounds.

Once you've read through a passage and figured out the punctuation, the next thing to do is to figure out why it's there. Don't worry about explaining every single mark. Instead, pick just one mark—ideally one that is used in several different ways—and focus on that.

For example, in this paragraph, we might want to focus on capitalization:

> On a dark December night in 1776, as he led a barefoot brigade of ragged revolutionaries across the icy Delaware River, George Washington said, "Shift your fat behind, Harry. But slowly or you'll swamp the darn boat." He was talking to General Henry Knox (they called him "Ox" for short). There's a painting of George Washington where he's standing up in a boat scanning the riverbank for Redcoats. I always thought he just wanted a good view. But I guess the reason he was standing was because he didn't have a place to sit down.

There are several different places where different kinds of words are capitalized. Let's see if we can figure out why:

EXAMPLE	WHY IT'S USED	QUESTIONS/COMMENTS
On...	Beginning of a sentence.	Sometimes I see really big capital letters, way taller than regular size, at the start of a story. What's that about?
December	Name of a month.	
Delaware River	Something that is one-of-a-kind. This is a specific river.	What if there's another Delaware River? Is that still one-of-a-kind?

George Washington	A person's name.	
General	A person's title.	Sometimes I see titles not capitalized. I don't understand how this works.
"Ox"	This is a nickname but I guess it's still a name.	
Redcoats	This is the name of a group of people.	

Even if you can't figure out why a mark is used, just trying to figure it out will help you learn. This is also a good time to go to one of those rule books you've probably got lying around somewhere. If you know the specific mark you want to learn about, and what you want to learn about it, a rule book can be useful.

Punctuation inquiry is just what it says it is: an exercise that involves inquiring into the use of punctuation. It's the questions, not the answers, that are most valuable. That's why the third column in our table is there. As you study punctuation, you'll find many situations where the way a mark is used differs from, or even contradicts, a way you've seen it used before. When that happens, write down your thoughts in the form of a question or a comment, and save it for later.

HOW DO YOU KNOW WHERE THE PERIODS GO?

If everyone knows to put a period at the end of a sentence, why are so many sentences missing their periods? Because even though we know what goes at the end, we often don't know where the end is.

Just about everything involved with sentence punctuation hangs on knowing where the end is. As we write, we give most of our attention to our words. Sometimes, however, they come pouring out so quickly that we push right on past where our sentences should end. When that happens, we have to go back and do a little detective work.

Let's see what we can do to patch up this little stretch of language:

> The sun is out today and the birds are singing there are children playing in the yard.

The first thing to do is read the sentence all the way through. We can tell by how confusing it is that there may be more than one sentence here. So let's go back to the beginning and start again, this time stopping as soon as a group of words makes sense:

> The sun is out

That makes sense; we could put a period here. But we don't know for sure if that's the end of the sentence, until we look at what's left over:

> today and the birds are singing there are children playing in the yard.

That's just as confusing as the sentence we started with. "The sun is out" can't be right. So let's go one word farther:

> The sun is out today

This works, too. But, just like last time, we need to check the words on the other side. We can call this approach "move and rock." Many times, when we're trying to split a long string of words into properly punctuated sentences, we have to move through them word by word and then "rock" back and forth over our potential period to make sure we've found the right place. "The sun is out today" sounds great. But when we rock ahead, we're left with this:

> and the birds are singing there are children playing in the yard.

A new sentence certainly could begin with "and." Despite what many teachers tell us, there's no rule against it. But as we read the rest again, it doesn't seem like we've found the right spot:

> and the birds are singing there are children playing in the yard.

So we need to keep moving ahead, one word at a time, until we find the next potential sentence end:

> The sun is out today and (Nope)
>
> The sun is out today and the (Nope)
>
> The sun is out today and the birds (Nope)
>
> The sun is out today and the birds are (Nope)
>
> The sun is out today and the birds are singing (Wait!)

Finally, we've come to something that sounds right: "The sun is out today and the birds are singing." Now, let's rock over to the other side of that period and see if what we have left works, too:

> there are children playing in the yard.

That also sounds good. We were fortunate to discover that we had only two sentences in that long string of words. Once we found the end of the first sentence, we were right at the beginning of the second:

> The sun is out today and the birds are singing. There are
> children playing in the yard.

That's perfect. ˊ

The "move and rock" strategy may seem a little tedious, but the more you do it, the faster you get. The important thing to remember is this: Just like crossing the street, you have to look both ways to make sure you're safe.

THERE'S GOT TO BE A BETTER WAY

If you don't like the "move and rock" strategy, there's another approach that involves paying close attention to the way we read. As we read over our writing, there are four expressive reading cues we can use to find the ends of our sentences. You know you've come to the end of a sentence when:

- **You come to a full stop.** When we reach the end of a sentence, we're supposed to take a little rest before moving on. If you feel like barreling on through, you might not be ready to pop a period in just yet. But if you're unsure, go back, read it again, and this time slow way down. We can fix a lot of our mistakes just by reading slowly. Keep one thing in mind: This has nothing to do with stopping to take a breath. I don't know why some teachers tell kids to put periods where they need to stop and take a breath.

Even when we read aloud, almost no one takes a breath after each sentence. And when we read silently, we don't breathe with our reading at all.

- **The words make sense.** This may seem obvious but it's not. As we noticed in our "move and rock" example, there can be many places within a sentence where the words seem to make sense. The trick is finding the right place. And sometimes that actually involves reading slightly ahead of ourselves.

- **Your voice slopes down.** There's a nifty thing that happens with the pitch of your voice when you read a sentence. It starts up high and ends down low. In most sentences, your voice will stay near the high level most of the way. Then, right at the end, sometimes in just the last few words, it'll tail off a bit, hitting its lowest point right when you reach the end.

- **Your voice slows down.** Right at the end of a sentence, as your voice slopes down in pitch, it will sometimes slow down a little, too. Be aware that we don't do this all the time. It's more likely to happen at the ends of longer sentences and when a sentence is the last one in a paragraph.

To notice these things, you have to read slowly, carefully, and expressively. You may even have to read your writing out loud. This expressive reading strategy is probably the best way to work with sentences because it forces you to use the same techniques your readers will be using to figure out your writing. But even the best strategy doesn't work every time. Most people use some combination of the expressive reading approach and the "move and rock" approach to get their sentences right.

Miss Margot says

Have I told you that I **love** reading my writing expressively **and** out loud? I **do**! First of all, it helps me find mistakes. Second of all—and this is the good part—it's hilarious, especially when I have dialog. Then I can **become** the characters. But even without other people's voices in the piece, I get a kick out of being expressive. See all these *italics*? I put them in so you could hear how I've been reading this in my head. (Mr. Peha is working, so I can't read it out loud.) **Shhhhhh**. It's so much fun!

SURPRISE ENDINGS

Of course, not every sentence ends with a period. Some end with question marks and an even smaller number end with exclamation marks. How can we tell the difference? Again, our voice is the best indication:

- **Up at the end quickly for a question mark.** Normally, when we get to the end of a sentence, our voice slopes down and slows down. In a question, we do exactly the opposite. At the end of a question, our voice quickly hops up a notch. (Some people will tell you to watch for "question words" at the front of the sentence like "What" or "Why" or "How." But that doesn't always work. Listening to your voice works every time.)

- **Straight up for an exclamation mark.** Occasionally, when a sentence we write is packed with feelings, or when we want to show that someone is shouting or is otherwise extremely excited, we punctuate the end of a sentence with an exclamation mark. When we read a sentence with an exclamation mark, our voice shoots straight up like a rocket. Some people are fond of using double (!!)

and even triple (!!!) exclamation marks. But there's really no such thing. One exclamation mark is all you get, no matter how much you want to exclaim. (Oh, and these are not called "excitement marks". If you throw them around every time you get excited about something, they begin to lose their punch.)

There's one last ending mark that very few people use. Yet it really does exist, and it really is quite useful. There's a situation in our language where a person is asking a question at the same time they are making an exclamation. For example, have you ever been with someone who does something a little dangerous all of a sudden? As they shoot off on their bike to jump over a creek, you might find yourself yelling something like, "Are you crazy?!" And there you have it—the *interrobang*. It's a combination of a question mark and an exclamation mark. It's the perfect choice when someone exclaims a question.

THE MUDDLE IN THE MIDDLE

Life at either end of a sentence is pretty simple. But in between, things can get a little crazy. For many situations there are no absolute right or wrong answers. So it's important to wade in with an open mind.

We know from Chapter 7 that sentences are made up of parts. We use punctuation in the middle of sentences to make those parts easier to read and understand. Just as we use periods at the ends of sentences to keep our ideas from running into each other, we use mid-sentence punctuation marks, like commas, to keep sentence parts apart. (Punctuation is all about separation. Every mark, except for the hyphen, is a separator of some kind.)

THE CANTANKEROUS COMMA

Cantankerous: difficult to work with or use. That pretty much sums up the comma. It's not really the comma's fault, of course. We humans have never been very responsible about the way we use them.

As you saw in the two examples at the beginning of this chapter, it's perfectly reasonable to write the same sentence with two commas or with no commas:

He felt the first blow on his back causing him to stumble and drop his bag which was promptly kicked into the bushes by another of the three.	He felt the first blow on his back, causing him to stumble and drop his bag, which was promptly kicked into the bushes by another of the three.

But while I might feel comfortable with either of these sentences, some people might argue that one is definitely right, that the other is definitely wrong, and that it's shamefully irresponsible of me not to teach you the difference.

This contentiousness over commas seems to be a permanent fixture in the world of writing, and I don't think it will ever end. If anything, it will only get worse as more and more people publish writing on their own, and cut out the editors, publishers, and academics who have traditionally been responsible for developing and enforcing the rules.

So, once again, you could find a rule book and learn to follow it. Just be prepared for the fact that the rules may change depending who your "ruler" is at a given time. What won't change, however, are the basic reasons why commas came into being in the first place. Below you'll find six things you can do with commas. Whether or not someone else wants you to do them is something you'll have to sort out when the time comes.

Putting rules and rule books aside for a moment, you can use commas to:

- **Separate parts in a sentence.** If you zip back to the section on sentence patterns in Chapter 7, you'll notice a comma in between the parts of every model and example sentence. I did this so you could learn about commas at the same time you were learning about sentence structure. This is exactly how commas should be learned because the most important use of the comma is to improve readability in complicated sentences by making sentence parts easier to identify. Out in the real world, you'll notice that many of these commas are now considered optional. Most commonly left out is the comma after an Intro part, or what some teachers might call an introductory phrase. Unless this part is very long, writers these days often skip the comma. For example, "All of a sudden the car in front of me swerved to avoid a huge box in the middle of the road."

- **Separate items in a list.** You probably know the argument about this one. Some people like to see a comma after the second-to-last item in a list; other people like to leave the comma off. This is called the "serial comma" issue. If you're like me, and you worry about your list items getting confused, you'll want the extra comma: "For breakfast I like Wheaties, Total, or Special K." But, to be honest, folks like me have pretty much lost this battle. Most people these days want a healthy low-fat sentence without unnecessary commas: "For breakfast I like Wheaties, Total or Special K." If you decide to adopt this more popular practice, be forewarned: There are situations where leaving off the last comma can get you in trouble. So drop it with caution and always read your writing carefully. Finally, whichever practice you choose, be consistent about it, at least within the same piece of writing.

- **Separate multiple modifiers.** Here's another big, fat, thorny controversy. If you want to describe a controversy that is big and fat and thorny, do you need to put commas in between each adjective? The traditional rule says you do. But many people will tell you that your sentence will read just fine like this: "Here's another big fat thorny controversy." On this issue, I sheepishly take the middle ground. If I'm using only two modifiers, I tend to skip the comma in between. But if I have more than two, I pop the commas in. Just like using the extra serial comma in a list, using all the commas in a list of modifiers is safer and clearer than leaving them out.

- **Separate things that might be confusing.** Commas are great for helping us avoid embarrassing moments like this: "The kids said they wanted to eat Uncle Jack before they went to the movies." Something tells me that Uncle Jack might appreciate a couple of commas: "The kids said they wanted to eat, Uncle Jack, before they went to the movies."

- **Separate speaking from speakers.** We use commas all the time in dialog, and whenever we're quoting something, to keep spoken words and quotations separated from other parts of our writing: "After that unpleasantness with the commas," Aunt Tilly informed us, "even watching movies at home makes your Uncle Jack a little nervous."

- **Separate information to make it easier to read.** Sometimes we use commas just to make things clearer for the reader. It's hard to tell at a glance that this number, 7000000000, is seven billion. But with a comma after each group of three zeros from the right, it's a piece of cake: 7,000,000,000. You'll also see commas used between days and dates (Tuesday, July 24, 1942) and cities and states (Carrboro, N.C.), among other places.

If you look at newspapers, magazines, and other contemporary information sources, you'll probably notice that commas are left out in many places where our rule books say they shouldn't be. Over the past 30 years or so, there's been a trend among professional writers—especially journalists—away from using commas unless they are absolutely necessary (like when your Uncle Jack won't come over to visit anymore, or when he gets nervous because Aunt Tilly ordered Showtime).

Miss Margot says

Guilty as charged, sir. I am one of those journalists.

Many writers feel that commas get in the way of the words and make reading harder than it needs to be. These writers prefer to make an extra effort to craft sentences that can be read reliably without commas. And while careful sentence crafting is always to be applauded, I'm going to recommend that you take a different approach, at least for the time being.

My advice to you about commas is this: Use them as much as you can while you're learning how to use them. Consistently separate the Intro, Main, In-Between, and Add-On parts of your sentences with commas. Include that last comma in a list, just as I did in the previous sentence. Separate all those adjectives. And be on the lookout for long strings of words between capitals and periods that you can break into shorter, more manageable pieces with a comma or two.

You're going to make a lot of mistakes with this approach. But you're going to learn a lot, too. Young writers often have a terrible time learning about commas simply because they rarely use them. That's what happened to me when I was in school and I don't want it happening to you.

THE DASHING DASH

Everybody loves the dash these days—except those of us who feel it's overused.

Now why did I have to put a dash in there? Wouldn't that sentence have read just fine without it? (Yes, a comma would have been great. For example: Everybody loves the dash these days, except those of us who feel it's overused.) So what's the deal with the dash?

The dash is supposed to be used to set off part of a sentence that you want to emphasize very strongly—like this! It literally dashes your reader's attention over to the part of the sentence that you feel is much more important than anything else. It's most frequently used at the ends of sentences like I've been using it here. But it can also be used in pairs if you want to bracket something important in the middle of a sentence like this:

> It seems that writers everywhere—and you know who you are—have taken to using the dash so frequently it is beginning to lose its value.

Miss Margot says

Mr. Peha is talking to me in this section, kids. I love to use the dash—especially in pairs—whenever it makes sense. Mr. Peha says I use dashes too often. He's always editing them out of my writing. But guess what? When he's not looking, I sneak a few of them back in before I send my pieces off to my clients.

Because the dash calls so much attention to itself, it's also used to signal an interruption, especially in dialog.

> "Mr. Peha," my English teacher shouted. "Why have you been using so many dashes of late?"
>
> "But Ms. Smith, I—"
>
> "There are no excuses, Mr. Peha!" she bellowed. "Never use a dash where a comma will do."
>
> "But—"
>
> "Silence! Your teacher has spoken."

Correct or not, the dash is certainly hip and trendy. So powerful is its allure that many of us go through a period of time when we use it for just about everything. Then we realize that the more we use it, the less useful it becomes.

Even though we don't think about this, every mark has a meaning. The dash means something like, "Hey, Reader, the stuff after the dash is a lot more important than the other stuff in this sentence. Pay attention." And it works, too. What reader can resist being rocketed down that line and crashed head-on into the next idea?

But just like the boy who cried wolf one time too many, those of us who are new to the dash tend to overuse it. Why? Because we want attention—precisely what the dash is designed to get us.

However, the more we use the dash, the less it seems to work. Soon, it stops working altogether. At this point, if we're smart, we cut back or stop using it for a while. If we're not so smart, we have no choice but to move on to the exclamation mark. Just remember: Using too many exclamation marks makes you sound like a breathless teenager whose every waking moment is drenched in drama and whose every thought seems like the most urgent insight ever.

Finally, you need to know this about the dash: there are two of them, one long, the other a bit shorter. The long one is called an "em" dash (—). The shorter one is called an "en" dash (–). The really short thing that looks like a dash is not a dash at all, it's a hyphen (-). On those rare occasions when you decide to use a dash, use an "em" dash; that's the long one. Don't use two hyphens (--). It looks amateurish.

Writing an em dash is easy. Just make a horizontal line a little longer than a minus sign. If you're working on a computer, however, typing an em dash can be tricky. If you're a Windows user, you have to first hold down the ALT key, then type "0151" on the numeric keypad, and then release the ALT key. If you're working on a Mac, it's a little easier. Just type SHIFT-OPTION-hyphen.

POLITE (OR IMPOLITE) PARENTHESES

You might find it useful to think of parentheses as the opposite of the dash. We use the dash to emphasize; we use parentheses to de-empha-size. If, instead of calling attention to something, you want to sneak it in at a lower volume level, parentheses are the punctuation mark for you:

> As I entered the classroom, I noticed that Mr. Funston was wearing mismatched socks and an unusually garish tie. (He must have dressed for school in the dark again.)

Parentheses are most often used for a type of remark called an "aside." An aside is a semi-secret comment. Imagine sitting next to a friend in class. You want to make a crack about Mr. Funston's clothes, but you don't want everyone to hear it (least of all, Mr. Funston). So you turn to the side, cover your mouth with your hand, and whisper, "He must have dressed for school in the dark again."

Parentheses are often used for humorous remarks. That's why you'll probably have occasion to use them most when you're trying to get a laugh. Like dashes, they are easily overused, especially when writers think they're funnier than they really are. (Come to think of it, you might have this opinion of me. But notice how I've de-emphasized this unpleasant thought by putting it in parentheses.) Of course, you can use parentheses to make a polite remark (Mr. Peha is a comic genius) just as easily as you can use them to sneak in something snarkly.

Miss Margot says

Mr. Peha wrote originally "snarkly" here but then his editor suggested "snarky" instead because it's much more common. But I like "snarkly" better so I'm sneaking it back in. After all, the only way we get new words in our language is by people using them.

THE COMMANDING COLON

There's no better way to describe the colon than this: It works like an equals sign. In almost every way that a colon can be used, you'll notice that the words on the left provide an equivalent description of the words on the right. For example:

> In this section, we'll be talking about six marks of punctuation: the comma, the dash, parentheses, the colon, the semicolon, and the ellipsis.

To the left of the colon, the description reads "six marks of punctuation." To the right are the names of the six marks. The colon is great for introducing lists like this. And that's probably the most common way writers use it.

But you can use the colon for another reason, especially when you want to emphasize an important point, because it really commands a reader's attention. That's why I used it in my first sentence about the colon:

> There is no better way to describe the colon than to say this: It works like an equals sign.

The commanding colon stops a reader dead in his tracks and, unlike the dash, holds him there for a moment, just as a period would at the end of a sentence, before allowing him to move on. And because it functions as an equals sign, the colon gives me a chance to tell the reader the same thing two times in two different but complementary ways. When you've got an important statement to make, something you want to be certain your readers understand, try the "commanding colon" trick just like I did, either at the beginning of a piece or right at the end. It's a perfect way to make a point your readers will remember.

Finally, there's the matter of whether or not we capitalize the first word following the colon. The official rule is this: When the words that follow the colon make up a complete sentence, the first word is capitalized. However, you may also have occasion to use a colon like this: to introduce a list, a series of short phrases, or a longer string of words that is not a complete sentence. In this situation, the first word is not capitalized.

THE SUPERFLUOUS SEMICOLON

Superfluous: more than is needed, desired, or required; not essential. And so it is with the semicolon. You can write your entire life and never encounter a situation where you absolutely have to use one. Anything you can do with a semicolon can be done with other marks of punctuation, or by simply adding or rearranging a few words. But semicolons are cool—*very* cool. And by using them, you will be cool.

The semicolon is the James Dean of punctuation, a true rebel without a cause. It knows you don't need it. And it doesn't need you either. It lurks in the lonely shadows between sentences that don't like being separated by a period and a capital letter. And it waits. Alone. It's not in a hurry. So don't use it. G'head. Stick with periods. Use commas. Throw in a conjunction. See what that gets ya.

The semicolon is the perfect punctuation mark to use when you want to show that there's a strong relationship between two complete, but otherwise independent, thoughts. For example:

> Nothing impresses an English teacher more than a well-used semicolon; no other mark of punctuation earns its user the same respect.

Now, there would be nothing at all wrong with writing that as two completely independent sentences:

> Nothing impresses an English teacher more than a well-used semicolon. No other mark of punctuation earns its user the same respect.

But the two ideas are so closely linked (you could probably put the word "because" in between them) that the semicolon is really the best way to go. If a period means, "This is the end of a complete thought," a semicolon means, "This is the end of a complete thought so closely related to the next complete thought that the writer couldn't bear putting a period and a capital letter between them."

THE ETHEREAL ELLIPSIS

Here we are at the end of our discussion of mid-sentence punctuation. And yet I feel there's something missing. Hmmm... Oh, yes, the ellipsis.

The ellipsis, or "dot dot dot" as some people like to call it, tells our readers that we've left something out. You'll see it used most often in quotations where the writer doing the quoting only wants to use part of what was said. For example, if you wanted to quote me on the use of the ellipsis, you might do it like this:

> According to Mr. Peha, "The ellipsis... tells our readers that we've left something out."

The stuff in the middle isn't absolutely necessary, so you'd leave it out and put an ellipsis in its place. This saves some space and keeps your readers focused on more important information.

In dialog, the ellipsis can also be used to show the passage of small amounts of time. For example:

> "Mr. Peha!" my English teacher yelled. "Where is your 5,000-word essay on the proper use of the ellipsis?"
>
> "Well... uh... you see, Ms. Smith, I...."
>
> "Silence!" she commanded. "I can tell by your ellipsis-strewn utterances that you haven't even started it."

Miss Margot says

Man, Mr. Peha's English teacher is very strict and formal. I wonder if he went to one of those fancy schmancy boarding schools where they call you by your last name and make you wear short pants and those jackets with the crests on them.

For some writers, the ellipsis seems to have the same addictive properties as the dash. People start using it and pretty soon they can't stop. If this happens to you, take a look at a novel or a newspaper article or something in a magazine, and see how often other writers use ellipses. It's not that often.

The other thing people like to do is add more dots. The thinking here is that if three dots means a brief pause, four dots could mean a slightly longer pause, five dots could mean perhaps pausing for 10 seconds, and so on up to a gazillion dots which means keep waiting until the universe collapses back into a quantum singularity—or the end of time, whichever comes first. While I like the logic here, I'm afraid I can't endorse this as good punctuation practice. The only time you'll see more than three dots in a row is when the fourth dot is a period that marks the end of the sentence.

Miss Margot says

If you want to make a newspaper or magazine editor wince, drop in an ellipsis or two when you're quoting someone. They don't like it because they think you could be leaving out something important—or worse—that you're bending the quote to make it say something you want it to that maybe it really didn't. So be careful what you leave out and make sure the omitted words don't change the speaker's true meaning.

MAKING SENSE OF THE MUDDLE IN THE MIDDLE

If you haven't already noticed, this section on mid-sentence punctuation is probably the longest section in this entire book. It's probably also the hardest material to understand and use. I've been writing professionally for almost twenty-five years, and I still struggle with this stuff. In fact, I know I'll receive dozens of corrections on my mid-sentence punctuation from my editor in every chapter of this book. (And dozens of complaints from teachers and editors everywhere on the advice I'm giving you.)

Learning how to use commas, dashes, parentheses, colons, semicolons, and ellipses is not something you can accomplish by zipping through a section of a book—even this book. Nor is this something you'll master one day and never need to worry about again. It's just that hard.

Believe me, I know how it feels. When I was in elementary school, I didn't get any of this at all. So for years, I wrote only short sentences. By keeping my sentences under ten words, I could get away without using any mid-sentence punctuation. But I couldn't write very much. And what I could write wasn't worth reading. By fourth grade or so, my thinking had outstripped my ability to punctuate my thoughts. So I just stopped writing altogether.

Don't let this happen to you.

I would have learned more had I taken more risks with my writing. If I had tried to use more marks, and then asked people for help when I was unsure of myself, I would have written more and, as a result, I would have learned more about how to punctuate.

The best way to make sense of the muddle in the middle is just to muddle through it. As much as I've told you not to overuse dashes and ellipses, I know that overusing these things, at least for a little while, is part of the natural way everybody learns. So go ahead and give it a shot. After all, you can't win if you don't play.

BE A WRITER LIKE LUCY LEDIAEV

Lucy Lediaev is a writer and web master at One Lambda, Inc., a medical technology company that makes test kits to match organ donors with transplant recipients. She writes technical instructions to help doctors and medical technicians administer the tests. In addition, she writes copy for marketing materials, content for the company web site, and software user manuals. In some ways, she's a "Jill of all trades," writing about a variety of subjects. In her spare time, Lucy enjoys blogging and writing humorous essays. She also writes web content for a site that focuses on kids.

Q WHAT KIND OF WRITER ARE YOU?

A Mainly, I'm a technical writer. I write about various aspects of technology. Most of my technical writing is in the computer software field or in biotechnology. I get to write about the latest technology and the latest discoveries in science. My primary job is to make complicated subjects simple. In a way, I'm a translator between scientists and people who don't have formal science backgrounds.

Q WHY DO YOU WRITE?

A I couldn't decide what I wanted to do when I grew up. I liked almost every field and found that I learned new subjects easily. I also like to teach and explain things to other people. I was fortunate enough to have some very good teachers in junior high and high school who encouraged me to write and who tuned up my writing skills with constructive criticism. When I was looking for a new career, technical writing was an obvious choice—I could write about things I found interesting and also explain difficult concepts to other people.

Q

WHAT MADE YOU WANT TO BE A WRITER?

A

I come from a family of readers. I learned to read and started to write before I began kindergarten. In school, I enjoyed writing compositions while my classmates were groaning about them. Even though I haven't been a writer in all of my jobs, I've always volunteered for tasks that require writing, because it was much more fun for me to write than to do routine tasks like typing and filing. I like using my brain and thinking critically.

Q

WHAT ADVICE WOULD YOU GIVE TO A FELLOW WRITER WHO WAS JUST STARTING OUT?

A

Read everything you can get your hands on. Then, write, write, and write some more! Keep a journal or blog in which you just let your writing flow without thinking too much about form. Also, learn the basics of grammar, punctuation, and spelling so you have the skills you need to write solid essays, stories, or poetry. Share your writing with people you respect, and ask them to critique it. Pay attention to what they say, and use their comments to improve.

A CAPITAL IDEA

Capital letters make up less than five percent of the symbols we deal with in our writing. But the effort we expend dealing with them makes them seem much more important than that. Of course, importance is exactly what capitalization is all about.

Back in the good old days, in the seventeenth or eighteenth centuries, for example, writers would capitalize just about any word they wanted. Everything must have been really important back then. Or maybe the few people who could write considered themselves to be really important. Either way, capital letters were sprouting up faster than cotton in the Carolinas. For example, here's an excerpt from a land survey report written by a young George Washington:

> By Virtue of a Warrant from the Proprietors Office I have Surveyed for Daniel Osborne a certain tract of waste and ungranted land on Potomack joining the upper Side of Daniel Pursleys Land & Bounded as followeth Beginning at two Ashes and an Elm on the river at Pursleys Corner and extended up the Meanders of the River.

Today, we'd capitalize only the names of the people and the rivers. But back in Washington's time, capital letters were used with reckless abandon. In most cases, writers used them on nouns. But here you can see that Washington even capitalized the verb "Surveyed." He must have thought the work he was doing was just as important as what he was doing it on.

Nowadays, we can't be so free and easy with our capitals. (Of course, if you know you're going to grow up to be the president of the United States, we can probably cut you a little slack.) Over the last 200 to 300 years, a wide range of customs has evolved regarding which words to capitalize and when. In my opinion, there are far too many capitalization rules now to make studying them even remotely interesting. So we'll just talk here about a few essential concepts.

ONE SIMPLE RULE, A MILLION COMPLICATED QUESTIONS

The standard rule about capitalizing things is this: Capitalize names, places, and things that are one-of-a-kind. I was in second or third grade when my teacher told us about this rule. At first, I was excited because there was only one thing I had to learn. But I quickly learned otherwise:

> "For example," my teacher said, "we capitalize the name of our school."
>
> "But what if there's another school with the same name?" I asked.
>
> "Its name gets capitalized, too," Ms. Smith answered.
>
> "But then its not one of a kind, right?" I said.
>
> "Silence!"

And later on:

> "Ms. Smith, do we capitalize the word 'hamburger'?" I asked.
>
> "No," she responded.
>
> "But I thought we capitalized names,"
>
> "'Hamburger' is not a name," she said with absolute confidence.
>
> "It's a name of a food," I cautiously suggested.
>
> "It has to be a specific name of something that is one of a kind," she insisted.
>
> "What if it's the hamburger from McDonald's that I ate yesterday?" I asked.
>
> "Silence!"

(You know George Washington didn't have to suffer through lessons like these. But I sure did. Maybe that's why I never became president.)

Knowing what to capitalize comes down to memorizing the long list of things other people have decided need capitalizing. I can never remember it all, so when I'm in doubt, I look it up or ask someone.

This is one situation where having a rule book can be helpful. (Although having a good editor, like I do, is even better.)

So rather than looking at a huge list of rules, many of which we'll never use, let's look at the three capitalization issues that come up for most of us on a regular basis:

- **The "Mom and Dad" Problem.** No, this doesn't have anything to do with how late you can stay up or how much allowance you get. It has to do with what you call your mom and dad and whether or not you capitalize the words "mom" and "dad." Check out this statement: "My friend calls his mom and dad Jane and Robert. But I call my mom and dad Mom and Dad." The first uses of "mom and dad" in both sentences are not capitalized because they refer to generic names for everyone's parents. The second uses of "Mom and Dad" are capitalized in the second sentence because I'm using the words "Mom" and "Dad" as the actual names of my parents.

- **The "Titles of Things" Problem.** The quick rule for capitalizing the titles of things is: "First word, last word, and all important words." But you'll see all kinds of different approaches out in the world. Applying the rule, however, will keep you from getting into too much trouble. For example: "The title of my story is *I Don't Want to Talk About It: How I Really Feel About the Rules of Capitalization.*" You can see that I kept the words "to", "the", and "of" in lowercase. But I capitalized "It" because it was the last word in the title. (The stuff after the colon is the subtitle; it gets treated like a separate title all its own.)

- **The "Titles of People" Problem.** This is a tough one, but it's really important because making a mistake with someone's title is almost as bad as making a mistake with their name. The basic idea is this: When the title comes before the person's name, and is actually a part of the name, you capitalize it; when it comes after, and when it's being used in a generic way, you don't. For example: "Attorney General Alberto Gonzales succeeded John Ashcroft as attorney general." Now, if I had ended the sentence with "...succeeded John Ashcroft as Attorney General of the United States," I would have used more capitals. Like the "Mom and Dad" problem, this one revolves around whether or not you're using the title like the name of a person (*the* Attorney General), or whether you're using it like a generic description (*an* attorney general). If you can't figure this one out, you can always Google it. That's how I got this example about Alberto Gonzales. I check all kinds of punctuation rules using Internet search engines. It's the fastest way I know to find out how different people do the same thing.

Finally, I want to say a couple words about writing with all capital letters: PLEASE STOP! I know it's very tempting to do this because I'm fond of doing it myself, as you just noticed. But it's not a good idea. Writing in ALL CAPS can be interpreted by your reader as shouting, and nobody likes to be shouted at.

If you want to emphasize something in formal writing, use bold or italics. In informal writing, like an e-mail, IM, or text message, put asterisks around important words like this: "This is a really *important* word." Better yet, in either formal or informal writing, just try to use more inventive—but still appropriate—language like we discussed in "Chapter 6: Better Words."

As for writing with no capital letters at all, I am not concerned, as so many adults seem to be these days, that this practice may hasten the decline of literacy, accelerate global warming, compromise national security, or promote moral turpitude among our nation's youth. In short, I just don't think it's a big deal.

When you're text messaging, for example, leaving off the caps makes sense for the sake of efficiency—and relief of sore thumbs. When you're IMing or e-mailing, all-lowercase writing looks and feels different than conventional mixed-case writing, so some people might say that it has a different meaning, too. If that's how you feel, and if that's the effect you're after, then it's a reasonable thing to do. Just do yourself a favor and keep the periods at the ends of your sentences. Your friends may be able to live without capitals, but you might throw them for a loop if they can't figure out where your thoughts begin and end.

IDEAS THAT BELONG TOGETHER

Think of a sentence as a single idea. Think of an entire piece as a large collection of single ideas—maybe twenty, fifty, a hundred, or even more. Now think of your reader having to slog through all those sentences, one after another, without even the slightest break every once in a while. That's why we have paragraphs.

WHAT A PARAGRAPH IS NOT

A paragraph is not five sentences. Or four or three or two or any particular number. Some paragraphs are one sentence. We see them all the time, especially in fiction and in the newspaper. A paragraph could be 143 sentences, but that might defeat the purpose of writing in paragraphs at all. For most writers, most paragraphs contain three to eight sentences. In general, novels tend to have shorter paragraphs; nonfiction books tend to have longer ones. Newspaper articles usually have the shortest paragraphs of all.

A paragraph is not something that begins with a topic sentence. Or something that has to have at least a beginning sentence, a middle sentence, and an ending sentence. There are really no rules about the types of sentences a paragraph must contain, although a paragraph has to have at least one sentence in order to be a paragraph.

A paragraph is not something that is only about one thing. Some paragraphs are barely about half a thing. Others seem to have two or three things in them. The number of things in a paragraph doesn't matter. What matters is that sentences relating to the same thing are grouped together. That's what a paragraph is—a group of sentences that are closely related.

A paragraph is not something that is indented. In some formats, we just skip a line between paragraphs. This is called "block" paragraphing, and it's used all the time in business writing, in technical writing, in e-mail, on the Internet, and in many other situations (like this book, for example). It doesn't matter whether you indent your paragraphs or not, as long as you're consistent about it within the same document. What does matter is that your writing has paragraphs, that they group your sentences together in logical ways, and that your readers can find and follow them easily.

A paragraph is not something you have to begin learning in third, fourth, or fifth grade. Kids in kindergarten and first grade are perfectly capable of creating paragraphs, just as soon as they create pieces of writing with sentences that can be put together in small groups.

A paragraph is not something you can get good at by writing them one at a time because someone tells you to. You only need to paragraph your writing when you have more than one. And the best way to learn to group your ideas into paragraphs is when the ideas you are grouping are your own.

A paragraph is not many of the things we are told it is in school. And the quicker we stop using English books, and starting using real books to learn about paragraphs, the better off we'll be.

THE BREAKS OF THE GAME

In a certain way, paragraphing is a lot like reading: Many people can do it but few can tell you how. Most people paragraph as they compose. We write a few sentences and then get this sense that we're about to start in on a new idea. So we start a new paragraph. Sometimes we go back later to touch things up—move a sentence out of one paragraph and into another, turn an unusually long stretch of sentences into two or three paragraphs—but mostly, paragraphing just happens for people. And if it's not happening for you, that's just the breaks of the game. Or is it?

While it's hard to learn to paragraph from other people, it's easy to learn from other people's writing. A few years ago, Miss Margot wrote an article for a magazine on a weird new kind of restaurant. When the article was published, it was laid out as one continuous block of text without paragraphs (left-hand column). But as you'll see, we can break it into paragraphs very easily (right-hand column):

Forget the little baggie of Cap'n Crunch you stash in your backpack every morning. The latest trend in fast food is cereal. The folks at Cereality stores in Philadelphia and Tucson stand ready to fill your bowl full of Frankenberry, Froot Loops, or Frosted Flakes. Pajama-clad Cereologists™ serve up your favorite hot or cold breakfast cereal in any combination you like. Mix Lucky Charms with Cocoa Puffs if you're so inclined. Or try the best-selling Life Experience™ blend featuring Life Cereal, sliced almonds, bananas, and a drizzle of honey. The standard serving is two scoops of cereal, one topping, and all the milk you can slurp for only $2.95. Just looking for a snack? Child size (one scoop, no topping) is $1.95. These people are so serious about cereal, they even have stylish "to go" bowls and boxes. After all, who wants to bop into first period bearing a box of Fruity Pebbles, inviting stares and snickers from friends? Co-founder David Roth says the company will open 12 more stores this year because, "People from all walks of life have personal bonds with cereal." Genius? Stupid? Who knows? They said nobody'd ever pay $4.25 for a cup of coffee, either.

Forget the little baggie of Cap'n Crunch you stash in your backpack every morning. The latest trend in fast food is cereal.

The folks at Cereality stores in Philadelphia and Tucson stand ready to fill your bowl full of Frankenberry, Froot Loops, or Frosted Flakes.

Pajama-clad Cereologists™ serve up your favorite hot or cold breakfast cereal in any combination you like. Mix Lucky Charms with Cocoa Puffs if you're so inclined. Or try the best-selling Life Experience™ blend featuring Life Cereal, sliced almonds, bananas, and a drizzle of honey.

The standard serving is two scoops of cereal, one topping, and all the milk you can slurp for only $2.95. Just looking for a snack? Child size (one scoop, no topping) is $1.95.

These people are so serious about cereal, they even have stylish "to go" bowls and boxes. After all, who wants to bop into first period bearing a box of Fruity Pebbles, inviting stares and snickers from friends?

Co-founder David Roth says the company will open twelve more stores this year because, "People from all walks of life have personal bonds with cereal."

Genius? Stupid? Who knows? They said nobody'd ever pay $4.25 for a cup of coffee, either.

The basic rule for paragraphing is this: Change paragraphs every time you change ideas. Of course, as we've seen, rules aren't helpful in every case—they are only guidelines. To paragraph a piece like Miss Margot's, we've got to decide where the ideas are. And sometimes that's not so obvious. So let's take a look at our paragraphing rationale and see how we did:

> Forget the little baggie of Cap'n Crunch you stash in your backpack every morning. The latest trend in fast food is cereal.

Changing from the introduction, which talks about the new trend in fast food, to the specific topic of the story, the new Cereality stores.

> The folks at Cereality stores in Philadelphia and Tucson stand ready to fill your bowl full of Frankenberry, Froot Loops, or Frosted Flakes.

Changing from the general announcement of the stores, to what happens specifically when you enter a store.

> Pajama-clad Cereologists™ serve up your favorite hot or cold breakfast cereal in any combination you like. Mix Lucky Charms with Cocoa Puffs if you're so inclined. Or try the best-selling Life Experience™ blend featuring Life Cereal, sliced almonds, bananas, and a drizzle of honey.

Changing from the kinds of cereal you can order, to the price you pay for a bowl.

> The standard serving is two scoops of cereal, one topping, and all the milk you can slurp for only $2.95. Just looking for a snack? Child size (one scoop, no topping) is $1.95.

Changing from the price you pay for a bowl, to additional information about taking your cereal to go.

> These people are so serious about cereal, they even have stylish "to go" bowls and boxes. After all, who wants to bop into first period bearing a box of Fruity Pebbles, inviting stares and snickers from friends?

Changing from taking your cereal to go, to a quote from the company co-founder about why they will be opening more stores.

> Co-founder David Roth says the company will open twelve more stores this year because, "People from all walks of life have personal bonds with cereal."

Changing from a quote from the company co-founder, to speculation about whether the restaurant is a good idea.

> Genius? Stupid? Who knows? They said nobody'd ever pay $4.25 for a cup of coffee, either.

Now, you may disagree with the way I've handled the paragraphs here. That's okay. There's usually more than one way to do it. Since this is a newspaper-style story, I tried to honor the newspaper tradition of using short paragraphs. But even if I chose to break the piece into fewer paragraphs, my point is this: Breaking long sections of text into separate paragraphs, or "smaller bites" if you like, is an effective way to make the reading—and the understanding—easier for your readers.

HOW DIFFERENT THINGS CHANGE DIFFERENTLY

If we were in school, we'd call Miss Margot's piece expository writing. When we paragraph most expository writing, we look for changes in the ideas we're using. This can be hard because it's not always easy to see where our ideas change.

Finding paragraphs in narrative writing is usually easier. In narrative writing, we can often rely on the sequence of events to let us know when things have changed. In general, when you're paragraphing narrative writing, you can change paragraphs every time you change action, time, or place.

Finally, changing paragraphs is part of writing dialog (which we'll cover in more detail in the next section of this chapter). The rule here is very straightforward and almost always works: Change paragraphs every time you change speakers.

EVERYTHING MUST CHANGE

As we grow up, we change. And so does our writing. In kindergarten, we may write only a few short sentences at a time. But in a little while, we're filling entire pages. Any time we write eight or ten sentences or more, we probably need to do a little paragraphing. This is because most of us tend to express our ideas in small groups of sentences.

In school, many kids avoid paragraphing, year after year after year. They just don't do it. Their teachers think they forget. But I remember back when I was that age, and I know exactly why I wasn't paragraphing: I was afraid to do it wrong, so I just didn't do it at all. Of course, not doing it at all was doing it wrong, so I wasn't getting anything out of pretending to procrastinate in my writing development.

But remember, your writing will change as you grow. And your use of punctuation will grow with it. The best thing you can do right now is to be thoughtful about how you experiment with paragraphing. When you see a big block of sentences staring back at you, begging to be split in two or three or four, don't hesitate. Just ask yourself, "What idea am I changing from?" and "What idea am I changing to?"

HE SAID, SHE SAID

Let's talk about dialog. It's not a difficult concept to wrap our heads around. Sometimes, in our writing, we want to show that people are talking, so we put quotation marks around the words they say. But, unfortunately, that's only part of the issue.

I'll tell you right now that I have a terrible time remembering how to punctuate dialog correctly. So whenever I have to do it, I reach over to my bookshelf, grab a novel, and see how someone else does it. This is a great strategy because, unlike many other punctuation practices, almost everyone punctuates dialog the same way.

TAG, YOU'RE IT

There are two important things to be aware of when we punctuate dialog: the quotation and the tag. The quotation is the collection of words actually spoken in the piece. The tag is the collection of words that tell us who spoke. For example:

> "I'm speaking these words," said the speaker.
>   QUOTATION   TAG

(The term "tag" is used by fiction writers. Journalists call it the "attribution." I call it the "he said, she said" part. But that's a little clunky, so I'm sticking with "tag" right now.)

TAG AT THE END

Normally, we quote the speaker first and pop a tag on at the end, like this:

> "I find punctuating dialog to be terribly tedious," complained Mr. Peha.

Notice the quotes around the words I am actually speaking, followed by the tag. But notice also that there's a comma inside the last quotation mark. This is used to further separate the quote from the person being quoted. Almost all additional punctuation marks like this will go inside the last quotation mark and not after it.

TAG AT THE BEGINNING

Though the tag normally goes at the end, it can just as easily come at the beginning, like this:

> Mr. Peha admitted reluctantly, "Putting the tag first always looks weird to me. But I know it's a good thing to do every once in a while."

Here, the tag comes first, followed by the quote. You'll notice also that a comma follows the tag (though sometimes writers use a colon) and that the quote is punctuated at the end with a period.

There's a tiny exception here that you need to be aware of. If the tag describes an action performed by the speaker within a complete sentence, we punctuate it with a period rather than a comma, like this:

> Mr. Peha slammed his fist on the desk. "This tag-at-the-beginning thing always gives me fits!"

I often mess this one up because I get so used to using a comma to separate the quote from the tag.

TAG IN THE MIDDLE

Just slightly more complicated is the situation where the tag falls in the middle, like this:

> "Of all the punctuation tasks," Mr. Peha lamented, "punctuating dialog is to me the most challenging."

In this situation, we treat the whole thought as a single sentence, quoting the exact words that were spoken and putting the tag in the middle of the sentence, surrounding it with commas, just as we would with any middle part if there were no quoted words at all.

Miss Margot says

I decide where to put the "tag" depending on the rhythm of the sentence. This is just another reason why writing like a reader—especially one who reads out loud—can be really helpful.

PUNCTUATION IN THE QUOTATION

Further difficulty in punctuating quotations comes from the fact that we have to punctuate two thoughts at the same time. Even worse is the fact that one thought technically lives inside the other. We often don't realize this until we have to punctuate a quotation that has its own ending punctuation:

> "Why is punctuating dialog so hard?" asked a distraught Mr. Peha.

In this situation, we use the normal punctuation from the quote's thought and leave out the comma before the last quotation mark because it would be superfluous. The rule in this case is simple: Never use more than one mark at the end of a quotation. So the following would be wrong:

> "Why is punctuating dialog so hard?," asked a distraught Mr. Peha.

If you look at it closely, it looks strange, doesn't it?

MORE THAN ONE SPEAKER

Of course, the real fun of using dialog is showing a conversation between two people. In this situation, all the same rules apply, plus we add one more: Start a new paragraph for each new speaker. Every time a new person talks, we give them a new line to start talking on.

> "Oh me, oh my. I seem to have such a terrible time punctuating dialog," said Mr. Peha in a weepy, self-pitying voice.
>
> "Nonsense!" said the English teacher. "You simply fail to apply yourself."
>
> "What does that mean, that I don't 'apply' myself?" asked Mr. Peha.
>
> "If you have to ask, Mr. Peha," the English teacher replied, "you are *certainly* not applying yourself."
>
> Mr. Peha rose from his desk in frustration. "Well, I'll just go look it up, then."

"See that you do, Mr. Peha," said the English teacher. "And heed the definition when you find it."

GRAB A NOVEL IF YOU NEED TO

Dialog is used so often in writing, especially in fiction, that even if you can't remember the right way to do it, you can always look it up in a book from your own bookshelf. Just turn to any scene where you find someone speaking. If you read far enough, you'll probably find an example of all the different ways of punctuating dialog that we've talked about here.

Miss Margot says

Newspaper and magazine articles can be good guides, too.

LOOK WHO'S TALKING

In this tiny piece about the beginnings of a new friendship, the writer, Ellie Davis, gives us a stretch of dialog without using tags of any kind. As long we can tell who's talking, tags are not actually needed—and neither is a lot of that messy punctuation we often struggle with.

Meeting Becca

We pulled into the driveway of our new house. At the house next door, a girl was on her bike, riding up and down the street. I was shy, six years old, and had only three playmates. Mom turned around from the driver's seat. "Ellie, how about you go see what that girl's name is?"

I looked out the window, then shook my head. Mom stopped the car, a signal that if I did not get out, I was dead meat. Reluctantly, I did as I was told.

I stood in front of the girl's path and waited for her to stop. Mom was watching me. I stuck out my hand.

"Hi," I said.

She frowned, but shook my hand. "Hi," she said back.

"Name's Ellie."

"Becca."

"OK."

"I'm free tomorrow."

"OK."

"Bye."

"Bye."

Nothing like a perfect conversation to get a friendship started.

Remember what I said about looking in a book of your own if you can't remember the rules for punctuating dialog? This tiny story actually has an example of almost every rule we just discussed.

Congratulations! You're a Better Writer

Author's Note

MAKING MY LIST

After I finish a big writing project, I like to think about how I did and what I got out of it. I think about the parts that I'm happy with and the parts that I wish had turned out better. If there are more of the former and less of the latter, I feel pretty good. And that's how I feel right now. But I also feel something else.

In this book, I've tried to show you how to be a better writer. And in the process of writing it, I think I've learned what I need to do to be a better writer, too. I've been writing since elementary school—professionally since college—but I still feel I've got a lot to learn. Here's my list:

Ten Things I Need to Do to Be a Better Writer

1. Say more, write less.
2. Understand completely how to use commas.
3. Use a higher percentage of shorter sentences.
4. Produce publishable pieces more quickly.
5. Be more disciplined in my use of pre-writing.
6. Develop a voice that is more mature.
7. Edit away from the computer with paper and pen.
8. Stop being satisfied with what comes easily to me.
9. Finish a piece of short fiction.
10. Always have a book in progress.

I make lists like these to keep myself focused on what's important. By putting my list here in the back of this book, I've now shared my commitment to becoming a better writer with thousands of other writers all over the world. That makes me more likely to follow through.

Why not make your own list? You can share it with your friends, your teachers, your parents. Or you can share it with me. Send it to mrpeha@beawriter.us, along with a few words about who you are and the kind of writer you hope to become. After I've looked it over, I'll write you back with advice and ideas about the things you want to learn.

To be better writers, we need to connect with other writers who are trying to be better, too. We need to share our successes and admit our failures. We need to support each other with new discoveries and important insights. We need to know that there are other people out there just like us, struggling with the same things we are.

So keep in touch. And let me know how I can help you to be a better writer.